HOW TO PASS EXAMS WITHOUT ANXIETY

In this Series

How to Apply for a Job
How to Apply to an Industrial Tribunal
How to Be a Freelance Secretary
How to Be a Local Councillor
How to Be an Effective School Governor
How to Buy & Run a Shop
How to Buy & Run a Small Hotel
How to Choose a Private School
How to Claim State Benefits
How to Communicate at Work
How to Conduct Staff Appraisals
How to Do Your Own Advertising
How to Emigrate
How to Employ & Manage Staff
How to Enjoy Retirement
How to Find Temporary Work Abroad
How to Get a Job Abroad
How to Get a Job in America
How to Get a Job in Australia
How to Get a Job in Europe
How to Get a Job in France
How to Get a Job in Hotels & Catering
How to Get a Job in Travel & Tourism
How to Get Into Films & TV
How to Get That Job
How to Help Your Child at School
How to Invest in Stocks & Shares
How to Keep Business Accounts
How to Know Your Rights at Work
How to Know Your Rights: Students
How to Know Your Rights: Teachers
How to Live & Work in America
How to Live & Work in Australia
How to Live & Work in Belgium
How to Live & Work in France
How to Live & Work in Germany
How to Live & Work in Hong Kong
How to Live & Work in Italy
How to Live & Work in Japan
How to Live & Work in New Zealand
How to Live & Work in Portugal
How to Live & Work in Saudi Arabia
How to Live & Work in Spain
How to Lose Weight & Keep Fit

How to Make a Wedding Speech
How to Manage a Sales Team
How to Manage Budgets & Cash Flows
How to Manage Computers at Work
How to Manage People at Work
How to Manage Your Career
How to Master Book-Keeping
How to Master Business English
How to Master GCSE Accounts
How to Master Languages
How to Master Public Speaking
How to Pass Exams Without Anxiety
How to Pass That Interview
How to Plan a Wedding
How to Prepare Your Child for School
How to Publish a Book
How to Publish a Newsletter
How to Raise Business Finance
How to Raise Funds & Sponsorship
How to Rent & Buy Property in France
How to Rent & Buy Property in Italy
How to Retire Abroad
How to Run a Local Campaign
How to Sell a Business
How to Spend a Year Abroad
How to Start a Business from Home
How to Start a New Career
How to Study Abroad
How to Study & Live in Britain
How to Survive at College
How to Survive Divorce
How to Take Care of Your Heart
How to Teach Abroad
How to Understand Finance at Work
How to Use a Library
How to Work from Home
How to Work in an Office
How to Write a Report
How to Write a Press Release
How to Write an Assignment
How to Write an Essay
How to Write Business Letters
How to Write for Publication
How to Write for Television

Other titles in preparation

PASS EXAMS
WITHOUT ANXIETY

Every candidate's guide to success

David Acres

Third edition

How To Books

AUTHOR'S ACKNOWLEDGEMENTS

In previous editions of this book I have been able to acknowledge a number of named individuals for their contributions. For this new edition, I am aware that not only have I had difficulty in keeping track of all those who have contacted me, passed on one sentence comments or mentioned something I thought could be useful, but space probably precludes a full acknowledgement too. However, I am able to acknowledge the contribution of my children-student guinea-pigs John Acres and Kate Acres, and offer thanks to Anna Fahdi, Tilly Kelly, David Leeper, Colin Richman, Suzanna Terry, Carol Turley and Katherine Turner for their contributions.

I am grateful to John Jenkinson who produced the initial line drawings in the anxiety section; Carol Acres for all her proof reading, comments and encouragement to keep writing and Asa Richman for her patient word processing of my handwriting as well as her enthusiasm for the ideas she read. My friends, particularly those in Barbican Counselling, were very helpful as I completed the manuscript, as was my colleague, Frances Prior.

My thanks to all of you who have contributed. I hope you feel something of the pleasure that I get from passing on these hundreds of ideas that enable people to gain the confidence to tackle coursework, revise, take exams, cope with anxiety, improve their memory and use helpers effectively.

British Library cataloguing-in-publication data
A catalogue record for this book is available from the British Library.

© Copyright 1987, 1992 and 1994 by David Acres

Published by How To Books Ltd, Plymbridge House, Estover Road, Plymouth PL6 7PZ, United Kingdom. Tel: Plymouth (0752) 735251/695745. Fax: (0752) 695699. Telex: 45635.
First edition 1987
Second edition 1992
Third edition 1994

Note: The material contained in this book is set out in good faith for general guidance and no liability can be accepted for loss or expense incurred as a result of relying in particular circumstances on statements made in the book. Educational regulations are complex and liable to change, and readers should check the current position with the relevant authorities before making personal arrangements.

Typeset by PDQ Typesetting, Stoke-on-Trent
Printed and bound by BPC Wheatons Ltd, Exeter.

Contents

Preface to the Third Edition   6

1   How to use this book   7

2   Tackling coursework deadlines   18
    Problem checklist p. 19

3   Organising your revision   39
    Problem checklist p. 40

4   Improving your memory   61
    Problem checklist p. 62

5   Taking exams   83
    Problem checklist p. 84

6   Coping with anxiety   107
    Problem checklist p. 108

7   Using others as helpers   146

    Glossary   153
    Bibliography   155
    Further reading and help   156
    Index   159

Preface

to the 3rd edition

Two of the most common reactions to the title of this book have been:

'Exams without anxiety – impossible, isn't it?' and 'Don't you need anxiety for taking exams?'

The thousands of students, teachers and relatives of students who have told me how well these ideas work in practice say that it is possible to take exams without anxiety, indeed many say they enjoy them because exams provide an opportunity for a 'performance' of what they know and understand.

I receive exactly the same message about *needing* anxiety. Whilst worry and excitement are part of preparing for any challenge, so is a calm inner world and a sense of focused readiness. You don't want to be caught in an anxiety state any more than you want to be so relaxed in the exam room that you are not ready for active engagement with the questions.

Gathered together in this book are hundreds of ideas to enable you to find a sense of balance so that any nervous energy you have will work for you rather than inhibit you. In this 3rd edition, there are over a hundred new ideas which include practical tips, checklists and examples of ideas that have worked for individuals. There are also two new chapters; one on Coursework and one on Memory.

Finally, I have incorporated into this book some of the more exciting ideas about how we learn and remember which have become more widely known in the last few years. I hope you enjoy trying them out. If you want to let me know if they worked for you, I would be very pleased to hear from you; my address is at the back of the book.

David Acres

1
How to Use this Book

Your starting point is to have five minutes to spare. If you really haven't, pick a better time. It is usually anxiety which causes you to feel that you haven't got five minutes; you probably have.

IN FIVE MINUTES or so, you can:

- read the back cover, the Preface to the 3rd edition and the list of contents
- use the time to spot whether the book appears to have some content relevant to you and to note chapters of interest to you
- jot down a question or two that you would hope the book could help you answer.

IN ANOTHER FIFTEEN MINUTES or so, you can:

- read the section **The importance of asking questions** (page 8), which is in many ways the most important section to understand if you want to make the best use of this – or any books and notes you read
- write down any question you have as you read through the **Problem Checklist**s or the chapters that seem most relevant
- note down useful tips as you find them in the checklists as well as the relevant page numbers. Then look up the relevant pages in the chapter.

If you can't find what you are looking for in the index, flip through the pages of the chapter(s) you feel are likely to be most relevant.

Keep your questions next to you and look for pages that may be relevant to them. Be methodical in writing down the pages you note as being useful looking.

You can use short bursts like this any time you visit the book with a particular question in mind.

THE IMPORTANCE OF ASKING QUESTIONS

I strongly recommend that you read through this book in exactly the same way as you should revise and take examinations – *with questions constantly in your mind.* Use these guidelines to develop your questioning techniques and then use them to *pick and choose the ideas which best seem to answer your questions.*

- Don't pick up this book after this moment without having a question in mind.

There are *two types of question* you should ask yourself continuously. The first type is about *the topic you are studying* eg The First World War if you are studying History as a subject. The second type of question is about *you*; what you are doing and how you are proceeding when you are studying. *Both types of questions are of equal importance.*

Questions about the topic you are studying

You can find questions about a topic you are studying from:

- Old examination questions. These are usually obtainable from an Examining Board or through teachers, lecturers or libraries.
- Questions you have tried to answer during the course eg essay questions.
- Any suggestions or guidelines given to you by teachers, lecturers or tutors.
- Talking to friends and sharing ideas.
- Your own interests, the thing you want to know.
- The work you have studied during the year, indicated by headings in your notes. You can convert these topic headings into questions by using questions beginning with the six key words in the Kipling poem, ie What? When? Why? How? Where? Who?

You would need to choose a topic and then see if you can think of a question beginning with any of those six words.

Example
Using the History topic, The First World War, I constructed six questions:

What... were the main causes?
When ....was the turning point of the war?
Why................................. were the casualties so enormous?
How............. was Germany made to pay at the end of the war?
Where................................. were the principal battlefields?
Who...... were the politicians principally responsible for the war?

You will need to construct the same sort of topic questions in order to use this book. Some useful questions about this book and the topics within it would include:

What problems have I got with studying for exams?
Why do I get so nervous and what can I do about it?
How can reading this book solve my revision problems?
Where should I revise?
Who should I use to help me – and how?
To what subjects do these ideas apply?
How difficult would it be to try this idea?
When should I start my revision?

Questions about what you are doing, how you are proceeding
These are questions you ask yourself in order to keep a watchful eye on how you are spending your time; whether you know what you are doing and why you are doing it. Some useful questions to ask yourself when using this book would include:

What am I reading this page for?
Why am I looking at this book?
What do I want to find out?
Where shall I look next?
Have I understood what I have just read?
When will I be justified in taking a break?
Am I concentrating?
What will I do immediately after I have finished this?
What is the time?

You will notice that not all these questions have to begin with the six key words. It is the principle of questioning that is, and has been, so fundamental in learning for hundreds and, indeed, thousands of years eg Socrates was promoting the value of question and answer in ancient Greece (Socratic dialogue). The particular value of it has been expressed well by Rudyard Kipling in 'The Elephant's Child':

I keep six honest serving-men
They taught me all I knew
Their names are What and Why and When
And How and Where and Who.

How to make up questions from printed or written materials
You can try this by opening any book and finding a *heading or sub-heading* on a page. I opened up this book and found the heading

Efficient revision (page 39) and tried peppering the heading using the guidelines from **The importance of asking questions**.

What makes for efficient revision?
How many features are there of efficient revision?
What's my most efficient time for revision?
When do I feel most efficient revising?
What is different to what I would do already?
Why change what I am doing already?

You can also use the *first or last sentence of paragraphs* to generate these types of question even when there is no sub-heading like 'Efficient revision'.

If you practise both of these techniques you will become a much more active learner. Then you can use the technique as part of your regular study habits whether during your coursework, assignments or preparing for exams.

Analysing the assignment question

The key to answering any question (even one you have set yourself) is to clearly understand precisely what it is asking you to do.

This usually means that you have to spend time, even slowly – analysing it *actively* by yourself, with a friend or both.

You can do this by the underlining technique shown on p 11 and you can couple this with a technique which I call 'peppering' or 'bombarding' the question with little questions. Some of these useful little questions are:

What does this mean?
How is this defined?
What is this?
Do I understand this?

Rudyard Kipling's 'honest serving men' also help (p 9).

To demonstrate this technique, I have both underlined and 'peppered' the question on page 11. As I did so, I spoke out loud talking to myself about each aspect of the question so that it was clear to me.

Having done this, I can use these 'little' questions to help me to set off with my reading. Later they will be helpful to enable me to structure the answer to the assignment. Initially though I can attempt to answer each question by jotting down my own first ideas, in a list, a spider-diagram or pattern. I can then go off and ask questions about other aspects of the assignment with some knowledge or understanding of my own with which to build a link – I can see an *association* between

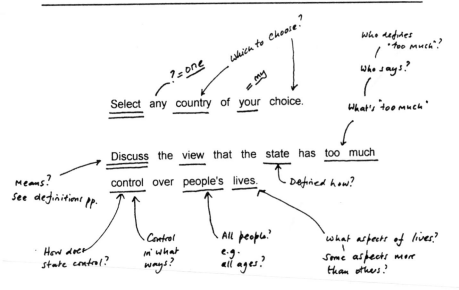

what I know and what I want to know.

- As an extra tip, carry cards, bookmarks or Post-its (see p 30) with these questions on, to keep you focused on the relevant issues when you are reading, thinking and note taking.

YOUR QUESTIONS ABOUT THIS BOOK

Who is the book written for?

Anybody, of whatever age, who is taking examinations at any level – school tests and examinations, GCSEs and A Level, Scottish Highers, Certificates, Professional qualifications, Diplomas, first Degrees and Post Graduate qualifications. It is also written for anybody who wishes to help the student study most effectively, eg parents, teachers and friends. **Using Others as Helpers** gives guidelines to both students and their helpers.

The ideas apply to any form of examinations – written or oral; word-based (descriptive); number-based (mathematical, problem solving) and multiple choice exams – taken in schools, colleges, Polytechnics and Universities. The basic principles involved in studying for all exams are the same.

What does it contain?

It contains dozens of ideas on how, when, where, how much, with whom and what to *revise*; how to prepare yourself for *examinations*; what to do immediately before and during the exams themselves; and how to cope with any *anxiety* you feel. You can discover exactly what it contains by reading the **Contents**; **How to use this book**; **A step-by-step guide**; **The importance of asking questions**; the five **Checklists** at the beginning of Chapters Two to Six.

Have I got time to read it?

Yes, definitely: half an hour well spent in reading parts of this book is very likely to immediately save you time. One hour spent extracting ideas from the book will give you a very clear picture of what the book contains and enable you to put effective ideas into practice immediately. Thereafter, five, ten or fifteen minute periods of dipping into the book for particular ideas to cope with particular problems will probably be all you need.

Do I have to read the whole book?

No. Select those parts that are relevant to your needs now and use them. You may never finish reading the book from cover-to-cover and that doesn't matter. Try, however, to form an outline idea of what is contained in the parts of the book you have not used. They may be useful later on. This book is designed to be used, not just read.

Where do the ideas come from?

They come from thousands of students I have worked with since 1970 when I began to work with individuals and groups of students to help them improve their studying. They come from two decades of being an examiner, originally at GCE O Level then at GCE A Level and subsequently for professional courses in higher education. They also come from the collective expertise of other authors of study skills, counselling and relaxation books and materials, whose work, wherever I have made direct use of it, is acknowledged. What we know about how we learn as the outcome of psychological research is also incorporated. Finally, the ideas come from teachers I have worked with both as colleagues and as a tutor on study skills courses for teachers.

Do the ideas work?

Yes. Every one of the ideas contained in the book has worked for some student, somewhere. The vast majority have worked for large numbers of students. I also use them – and did so to write this book as I describe in **How did I write this book?**

Do I have to follow all these ideas?

Definitely not. There is no one perfect or correct way of revising or taking examinations. There are numerous ideas that work. Pick and choose those ideas you feel would suit you and your needs. Add them to any ways you have for studying already that you want to retain.

It is worth noting that it is often difficult to change your old habits, your old ways of doing things. Even if they don't seem to work very well, at least they are known to you, familiar, ie 'The devil you know rather than the devil you don't know'. My experience is that it is worth changing at least some of your old ways. It is likely you are already using some of the ideas in the book if you are studying effectively. If you are not using any of the ideas in this book, I'd be very surprised if you are studying effectively.

Bear in mind that new ideas often need a little practice. Sometimes, like any new skills, your performance may be less effective for a very short time, before you see the real benefits. Having said that this may occur, the opposite is true of many of these ideas: you will see immediate improvement in performance.

If I've got the ability, do I need this book?

You may not. Ability, hard work and determination have seen thousands of students successfully through the exam system – but not necessarily. Anxiety affects people of all abilities. Among the people I have met who are most anxious about their examinations are large numbers who have gained Upper Second class and First Class Honours degrees.

There is a belief that those who do well in examinations are those who have ability, work hard and are determined characters. Expressed as a sum, it would be

ABILITY + DETERMINATION + HARD WORK = ACHIEVEMENT

I would have difficulty in marking this sum, as I believe it is incomplete. Correct as it may be for many candidates, it is certainly inadequate as an explanation of the achievements of many others.

Two examples of this are:

- Those whose ability appears to produce achievement without hard work or determination. This is a category of candidate who is often referred to, but is, I suspect, less common than supposed. This candidate makes others feel sick!

- Those whose determination and hard work overcome their apparent lack of ability. In my first year of teaching I met Charlie, a year Ten schoolboy who had a measured IQ of 71. He later successfully took Science O levels, A level Chemistry and went on to Higher Education. As at the time it was supposedly a borderline decision as to whether he then went to a special school or not, this *both* demonstrated to me the value of absorbing interest, hard work and determination *and* commented upon the value of summarising a human being's ability to learn by a number.

The five factors of achievement

I believe that *Achievement* is not the sum of three but five factors. They are:

1. *Ability*

Whilst there are obvious limits to an individual's ability to achieve in particular areas of activity, I believe that much ability of the most able to the least able, remains untapped and under developed. Further, I believe most candidates can considerably improve their performance in examinations and that the vast majority who are entered for a particular exam have, at the very least, the ability to *pass* it. With better *technique*, most candidates would be gaining more marks.

2. *Determination and motivation*

Determination is a very useful trait, if it is channelled and focussed in the appropriate direction. I have met very determined people who have striven in entirely inappropriate ways and as a result exhausted themselves and marred their exam performance. However being motivated to do this for yourself is an extremely important part of successful study.

3. *Work rate*

I've met large number of candidates who have worked very hard but inefficiently and whose performance in examinations has been a surprise and disappointment both to themselves and their teachers, families and friends. Hard work should bring achievement when coupled with efficient and appropriate revisions and exam techniques. Indeed most students should be able to achieve satisfactory standards without hard work, if their techniques are good.

4. *Techniques*

Here I am referring to the contents of this book.

5. *Coping with yourself as a person*

Success in examinations is not just a matter of using your thinking or intellectual ability. It is also dependent upon your feelings and behaviour. In particular how you cope with the potentially bewildering tasks you aim to complete; how you cope with any past experiences of learning and taking exams (frequently negative); how you cope with your own or other people's expectations and how you cope with any anxiety you experience, are often just as important as ability. This is the reason for a **Coping with Anxiety** section being incorporated with **Organising Your Revision** and **Taking Exams** in this book.

My revised sum would be:

> ABILITY + DETERMINATION + WORKRATE + TECHNIQUE + COPING WITH YOURSELF = ACHIEVEMENT

What makes this different from other books on studying for examinations?

It is very comprehensive. It does not moralise and tell you what you ought to do or give you lots of 'good advice'. It is clear and straightforward to use. As it tells you how to use the book, it cuts down on the amount of time needed before you put the ideas into practice. It combines revision and examination techniques with ideas for coping with your whole lifestyle including any anxiety you may feel, to help you become a really efficient student.

How did I write this book?

I used many ideas in this book in the process of writing it. Using the six question approach (Why? What? How? Where? When? Who?) — this is how I did it. You may find some ideas are relevant to you as you tackle your revision or project.

WHY did I use particular approaches to writing?

I chose techniques which suited my particular way of doing things. I had to find ways of using short periods of time to 'nibble away' at parts of the book as well as find a way of keeping together all the ideas I was collecting. I did not want to lose any.

There were new ideas I wanted to understand, so tried them out as I wrote.

WHAT were the key approaches I used?

For my key approaches, I:

- watched out for ideas in television, radio, magazines, newspapers, books and videos. I grabbed a piece of paper and wrote down the key ideas immediately.
- noted new ideas as I heard people talk about them
- broke the whole task down into bits – chapters and parts of chapters
- used Post-it notes to record all types of information such as quotes,

page references, things I wanted to re-write
- took lots of breaks for fresh air, stretching my arms and legs and talking over what I had achieved
- listened to music (Mozart, Jon and Vangelis et al) and went for swims or walks.

HOW did I use the material I had gathered?
As key methods, I

- kept all the materials I gathered in separate transparent plastic envelopes which I labelled with Post-its stuck to the front sheet inside, eg 'MEMORY'
- used paper clips to keep similar types of ideas together
- stuck Post-it notes on sheets of A4 paper and rearranged them so that they made sense, if necessary moving them to separate sheets of paper
- put all of the book materials in one filing basket, in one place, so I knew where it all was
- when in the final stage, spread the materials out in neat piles all over the room in which I was working
- made connections of new material with the existing material, checking how one fitted with the other
- collected all the ideas and material onto one sheet of A3 paper in a patterned note.

WHERE did I find the best places to write?
I wrote it in:

- many different places. This was written on a Post-it sat on a bench in the grounds of an hotel initially and then finished in the hotel bedroom at a desk in front of a window.

I also wrote it:

- in my study/lounge at home sat at a desk which was cleared except for the pieces of paper needed to write that particular section. A lamp to one side of the desk shed light in the right place. I wrote in pen or pencil
- in Darlington public library when I visited the town: some sections which required reading new ideas were helped by the quiet reference area atmosphere
- whilst at a conference in Ripon in a students' study bedroom (during their vacation)
- in a number of outdoor locations when I noted things on cards or Post-its which I later transferred to a file and, even later, onto a sheet of A4 paper

You can check out your best places in **Check out your study environment.**

WHEN did I write the book?
- Over a long period of time – years of collecting ideas on pieces of paper: some parts were completed two years before it was published, some the day before the manuscript was complete
- mostly in the morning, sometimes early and sometimes late at night (see **Your best time of day**)
- at all seasons and times of year but with bursts of activity lasting several weeks when I wrote more intensively and regularly, putting together the original material.

WHO helped me write it?
- me, in general, once I had found the best ways to write, I was helpful to myself. I did most of the things that I needed to do for me. See **Be kind to yourself** (page 23)
- my family who gave practical help
- all the people who contacted me and told me what had worked for them – they are recognised in the Acknowledgements and Preface to the 3rd edition.

2
Tackling Coursework Deadlines

THE CHALLENGES OF COURSEWORK

It is not just exams which can generate anxiety when you are studying. Many students are finding that coursework and coursework deadlines can be just as difficult to manage. There can be problems in tackling several assignments for different subjects at the same time. Projects can prove difficult to start and/or to complete. In further and higher education you can meet up with tests at the end of short courses or modules, which count towards your overall diploma or degree performance.

From GCSE onwards, more courses in sixth forms, further and higher education have coursework as an important component in the overall assessment. The percentage of coursework marks that count in the final assessment can vary from 100% to 0%. 40% is a common average, although in subjects like English and Mathematics at GCSE level that percentage is likely to be no more than 30% or 20%.

There can be many problems to overcome when tackling coursework and the Problem Checklist on p 19 can help you identify the parts of this chapter and other chapters which can help you solve them.

But do not despair – problems are there to be overcome and here you will find dozens of ideas that other students have used to successfully meet coursework deadlines. The key solutions are often to do with how you organise both your time (when) and your place (where) of study, and here you will find ideas about both.

TACKLING THE PROBLEMS OF COURSEWORK

Have you left it too late?
Even if you feel you have left the coursework until too late, you probably have not as there are normally still some marks to be acquired. Providing you have not missed firm deadlines beyond which

Problem Checklist

I have/may have problems with	Tick if it applies to you	Brief tips	Where to find out more
Leaving coursework until the last minute		Avoid running scared. Spend a few minutes – 5 or 10 – doing some small task connected with different coursework for a few days, it soon mounts up.	20-21
Getting started		Start at a time you're most alert and most relaxed picking something you find interesting, easy or understandable.	20-24
Organising myself		Find some permanent shelves or storage space for your paper; colour code what you want to find.	26-27, 31
Motivating myself		Give yourself specific rewards for completing a short easy or interesting task; work with a friend; change time and place to study.	21-22 50-54
Falling behind with a project		Talk over with someone what the problem is – identify it and start to nibble away at the separate tasks that make up a project or dissertation.	28-30
Organising my room		Do not work in a tip as you will probably feel messy; look at it afresh, move things around so it feels as right as it can.	26-27
Friends interrupting me		Opt for friends who cheer you up when they phone or call; negotiate some nights or time for study/some for social life – and remind them you both agreed.	125-126 147-148
Meeting deadlines		Keep dates pinned up on a board.	34, 36-37
Falling behind with coursework		Divide time up between subjects, ticking off your time progress. Identify problems or blocks and seek help by changing your approach.	51-54
Balancing the amount of work I do for each subject		Tick off your progress in each subject, matching up the number of ticks.	51-54
Panic		Do a little often, talk to someone who you find helpful about your worries; learn some techniques to stop panic.	29-30 107-145
Forgetting deadlines until the last moment		Try a wallchart with dates clearly indicated.	34
Deciding which coursework to tackle first		Use a simple prioritising system such as that used for revision; do not use urgency as the only deciding factor.	43-44
Finding the best time of day to study		Check the exercise provided and try to spot both your first and second best times of day (so you have a choice).	33-35
Finding enough time to study		There are 168 hours in a week, plenty of time for you to find around 20 hours spread over 7 days.	52-53
Finding the best place to study		Use the environment checklist to spot your best learning environment.	25-26

no marks can be obtained, you can rescue something from the mess you may feel you are in by a basic approach which means you:

- *Do something.* The time for worrying is past; here is an opportunity to get on with it so take simple practical action such as find some facts; speak to someone; collect a book; talk to a tutor; photocopy some useful pages from a book and so on.
- Cut out the frills or anything but the essentials in what you write ('Cut the crap').
- Decide on a clear line of approach – and stick to it.
- Use the **Deciding priority** list (p 43) to decide a starting point. Start with areas of highest appeal and that are most useful.
- Break the whole assignment down into 'bite size' bits or 'nibbles': tackle these one at a time.
- Pursue the answers to one or two vital questions, putting the other questions to one side initially.
- Write in short simple sentences, wasting the minimum time in forming words.

Ready to study?

You can waste a lot of time at a desk trying to study unless you approach it in the right frame of mind. The following eight point plan will help you check whether you are properly prepared to start out on an effective study session. (You can find a patterned note version of the points on page 49.)

1. Are you relaxed and composed?
Avoid starting at the task in a state of anxiety. There are a number of suggestions for preparing yourself in the **Coping with Anxiety** chapter but a positive frame of mind, some physically relaxing movement before you start and some background music may all help.

2. Are you wanting to do it?
Check your motivation out by using the guidelines in **Motivating yourself**. *Wanting* to be studying that particular topic is a key to starting doing so.

3. Are you clear about what you are going to do?
You are ready when you have a specific one, two or three tasks in mind and some sense of the time scale attached to them, ie 'I will X by Y time'. Do not set artificially strict deadlines on yourself, for that way you may end up with a sense of failure, rather than success.

4. Have you got your questions ready?
This is to emphasise the point that we learn best those things that are answers to questions and that having a question or two in mind provides a valuable starting point. See **The importance of asking questions**.

5. A 'feel good' place to study?
Feeling right about the study environment will enable you to settle to the task quickly, particularly if you have cleared the space of clutter. You can check out your best learning environment on pp 25-26.

6. Gather the material you need
Having the books, newspaper articles, handouts, notes, drawings, calculator or tape recorder by your study space will enable you to make a start, confident that you have sufficient reference material close at hand. This also assumes that you have familiarised yourself with how to use a library and other electronic equipment that can help you find or use material. If you have not, then identify what you need to know and ask someone with the know-how to show you the practical steps you can take. If you build up your confidence in information gathering, it will spread to other study tasks.

7. Pick the right time of day
Some routine tasks that require little concentration or energy fit into your low-energy times of day once you have identified them. Thus, sorting out your folder, making a list of things to do, tidying your desk, phoning a friend to clarify a point or photocopying some notes you need can occupy the low-energy points, whilst creative tasks like writing, problem solving or designing can occupy high-energy times.

8. Use people in the right way
If you have made the best use of people to help you prepare to do the part of the study task you are now tackling, you will be happy to work on it by yourself. However, if you feel that you would still like to clarify some aspect of the task or gather some more information from a tutor or friend, then that becomes your first study task. It means you are ready to study by picking their brains (which is part of an effective approach to coursework).

Motivate yourself
There are a number of ideas you can use to improve (or even find any!) motivation:

- Talk about what you are worried about with friends or an objective outsider such as a tutor or counsellor.
- Remind yourself of what you are doing 'it' (the study task) for, keeping your dream and goals in mind.
- Picture yourself doing it well and enjoying it.
- Pin sheets of paper on the wall.
- You can pin up A4 sheets of paper in front of you as reminders.
- When you are flagging or unmotivated you can look up and remind yourself what you are doing. It helps keep you focussed on an assignment, a revision topic or why you are bothering to study at all.

I WANT TO BECOME A P.E. TEACHER	HOW HAVE LEISURE PURSUITS CHANGED IN BRITAIN SINCE 1945?
ie, *Why* are you studying	ie, *What* you are doing eg, the assignment question the revision question.

- Get away from it purposefully – not to escape because you are avoiding tackling tasks – but because you know you need to do something entirely different so as to come freshly to a task.
- Remind yourself of a feeling of well-being or good achievement you had in the past. Go inside yourself and make a picture of what you were like, how it felt – the total sensation of that moment. You can use this same exercise later to help build your confidence for revision. In the same way, you can picture yourself having successfully completed the tasks ahead, how it felt and what other tasks you overcame before you tackle the coursework.
- Think and talk positively. Avoid saying to yourself, 'I must get down to it' (a common phrase). See also **Talk positively** below.
- Use your best times of day to study (see p 33)
- Find and use the best place to study – one which 'feels' right and try also to find an alternative, second best, place (see p 25).
- Be imaginative in the type, variety and frequency of the rewards you offer yourself.

Talk positively

As you look at the two columns of phrases listed below, spot the words you say to yourself when you are tackling any coursework assignment or deadline. See if you can circle the words you use most often.

I want	I must
I like to	I should

I will	I ought
I need to	I have to
I am interested in	They told me to
I am going to . . .	I was told I must . . .
I will do (task) by (when)	

If you find yourself circling some words on the right-hand column, see if you can shift yourself to words in the left-hand column; for on the left are the words that are more likely to motivate you and enable you to complete tasks. The words on the right are emotionally value-laden and oppressive in feel; they are less help in motivating yourself.

Be kind to yourself

Most of all, to motivate yourself, be kind to yourself. When people say 'Do you think I should push myself harder?' or 'I get tough with myself' or 'I force myself to do it', I often want to ask: 'Are you sure that is the way to motivate yourself?' Sometimes the answer is 'Yes, it is'. In which case, and you really know yourself well, that is fine. However, most of us will not sustain our motivation to study over a period of time by continuously being hard on ourselves or by forcing and pushing. The answer to many study tasks is not to beat yourself up for failing to do things but to reward yourself for doing something positive and constructively – however little the task. Thus it is helpful to treat yourself kindly or 'softly and gently' by

- relaxing into what you are doing
- listening to music that aids your concentration (do not fool yourself on this)
- enjoying the rewards
- looking forward to whatever it is you are going to do
- enjoying the time, place and atmosphere to the full
- seeing time off, fun, sport and exercise, social life and time outside of study tasks as part of effective study, part of the balance of life.

Get the balance right

If you get the *balance* right, you will be more energised for the study tasks. The people of Trinidad and Tobago have the word 'to lime'. If you are 'liming' you are doing nothing much; hanging around with friends; having something to eat and drink; sunbathing; taking things easy. Talking to 1300 fourteen to eighteen year olds in these two Caribbean islands, it was clear that the most successful students had the ability to both work and play, or were successful at study because they knew how to use the ideas in **Be kind to yourself**.

You can deceive yourself or deliberately lie to yourself about whether you are getting the correct balance between work and play. It is my belief that you will know when you are fooling yourself. You can get it wrong by overworking or over-playing but one thing is clear to me from the experiences of tens of thousands of students I have spoken to on this issue — *that time away from tackling coursework assignments or revision is part of effective studying, not a separation from it.*

Finding it difficult to sustain your energy?

Even when you are tackling study tasks at your best times of day you may still find it difficult to sustain your energy. You can try the ideas in **Improving your concentration** (below) to maximise the use of the energy you have.

Improving your concentration

Improving concentration and your energy level is frequently *either* a matter of using more effective study approaches *or* resolving a personal concern which is interfering with your study. In the latter case, talking to someone may help, eg a friend, a relative, a teacher, doctor or counsellor, as described in **Using Others as Helpers**.

The following study approaches will aid your concentration:

Find a place to work which has a good feel to it
It should be a place that has enough light, heat and space around for books and papers. It should be a place you like to be.

Have all the materials you need assembled around you from the start
Don't give yourself an excuse to postpone starting.

Devise questions
to which you seek answers, as described in **The importance of asking questions**.

Be active in what you do
eg speak aloud, tape record, talk to someone, write notes.

Pick topics to study which you already understand and
find most *easy to tackle and* are of most *interest* or use to you as well as those which are particularly *useful* or *urgent*. Specific ideas are given in **What should I revise?**

Set yourself realistic small targets
This will give you more chance to succeed in reaching your goal. Success will increase both your self confidence and your work rate.

Vary
both the topics you study and the methods you use.

Study for short periods of time, at least initially
15, 20, 25 and 30 mins. can be very effectively used on routine study. Short breaks can be used constructively either for relaxation or recalling what you have been doing.

Rest and relax
Be positive about your breaks from study. Give yourself a day off a week at least and other free time when you are not obliged to feel guilty. A drink or a favourite television programme can be used as a reward for the completion of a specific study unit. Physical exercise, eg a walk, a run, a swim, yoga exercises or team games can help revitalise you, much studying is relatively passive.

Check your sleep
Lack of concentration is often due to failing to look after a basic need for sleep. **Getting to sleep at night** offers several ideas to help those with this difficulty (p 123).

Check your study environment
Where do you like to do your coursework? You can use these questions to help you locate your best place of study – but notice some tasks are better performed in some places than others.

Check your place to study by asking yourself these questions:

Which rooms or spaces suit you best?
eg Bedroom, kitchen/dining room, study, lounge, library, classroom?

Do you use chairs?
eg Sat upright at a table or an armchair? Lying on the floor or bed?

What rewards do you give yourself?
eg Special food and drink, TV programmes, going out and meeting friends?

What atmosphere do you need?
eg An open window; a very warm room; a desk lamp, fluorescent light; natural daylight?

What sound do you need?
eg Complete silence; some background music or sound; headphones?; types of music?

What do you need in your surroundings?
eg Books and papers assembled around you; a clear desk; papers on shelves nearby; TV on or off?

Do you need a specific view?
eg View out of window; posters or pictures; pinboard or noticeboard near desk?

Do you need people around you?
eg Someone in the home; work with another person (who?); best by yourself?

Can you study outside – in all seasons?
eg Can you study in a car, on a walk or sat by a stream or sea in any season of the year?

Organise storage space for notes and books

I know from my own experience that so much time is wasted if I do not know where to find some notes I need to work on. It is not just time that is wasted, it is nervous energy too. I am often anxious about whether I am going to find what I am looking for; it delays getting started on the study task and I often have a sense of unease (a sort of mental unpreparedness) if I do not know where things are to be found.

Thus a place or places where you can leave your notes and books is an essential aid to completing coursework assignments for deadlines.

If you have not got such a place, ask for and negotiate some space in your home where you can leave things *undisturbed*; having to scoop up all your papers into a mixed up pile again is one of the particular time wasters.

If you are unable to leave things undisturbed on a table or desk then a bookcase or wall shelf is equally helpful. Alternatively you could keep subjects in a particular place in a room or rooms, thus psychologically separating out subjects. Sometimes a filing cabinet drawer or portable file can be usable for this purpose, with file dividers for subjects, topics and, particularly usefully, the date order of coursework deadlines. In them you can keep the relevant material you are working on.

Whichever system you set up, keep an *index* or *catalogue* of what you have got where. It can be as simple as a sheet or two of A4 paper at the front of your ringbinder. It may also be a card index or you may keep it on a computer, onto which you have the option of entering your notes too. It will help you to remind yourself where to put things and find them.

You can colour code the areas and files too, eg the yellow area is English; the red is Maths.

It is particularly useful to find a place where you can leave the coursework assignment that you are currently working on, so that you can resume tackling the task with no wasted time or energy.

Keep on top of your folders and portfolios

In GCSE you have folders and in further or higher education you have portfolios. In them you place the completed essays, assignments, reports, drawings, designs, laboratory write-ups, fieldwork notes and all the other tasks you have been asked to complete over the course of a year or two. They are used as a method of assessing your effort and achievement over the course.

Folders and portfolios can become a mess. Typically, you may stuff assignments into a folder when you have finished them and they have been marked – and then forget about them. To avoid last minute panic and effort you can attend to them as the time passes by:

- re-writing illegible material
- keeping the assignments in order and in plastic envelopes, when appropriate, to keep them undamaged and clean
- re-checking material for easily-corrected errors
- keeping it in a safe place, where it will not get lost or dog-eared
- reviewing the material in the folders ie check it for understanding and asking yourself questions about it. Building up reviews of your work is a key principle in learning and will make the revision period easier when you have developed this reviewing habit.

Starting a learning journal

This is a type of diary in which you can record your own thoughts on your studying for yourself on a regular basis, in short bursts. It can either be a book or a loose-leaf folder.

You could use it for a variety of purposes.

- To recall and capture something you have just seen, heard and understood that day.
- You can use it to help build your confidence in what you now know or have just understood properly, perhaps for the first time.

- To ask yourself, 'What – if anything – did I learn today?'
- To moan to yourself about those things that frustrate you, confuse you or worry you.
- To list questions that are still unanswered and you want answered.
- To list words you want to look up in a Dictionary or Thesaurus to check their meaning.
- To connect something you have been doing on your course with something that has happened outside such as
  - a conversation with a friend
  - an item on the news or a TV programme
  - an article in a magazine.
- To make lists of things to be done.
- To write a letter to an imaginary or real friend which explains your ideas, thoughts or lists your questions about a topic.
- To comment on how you feel your contributions to a class were received.
- To give yourself a pat-on-the-back for achievements, using it to encourage yourself.
- To record the times of day and places you studied and how well it went.

This way you can spot a pattern of effective study times more easily. The 'windows of time' exercise can also help you identify your best times for study.

Overall it should be an enjoyable task to keep a journal; it need not take up much time on a daily or weekly basis, although sometimes it will feel an effort to write in it. Overall a journal should not take more than ten minutes a day and it will be enjoyable to do.

As one American student wrote: 'This was my first experience of writing a journal and I have to admit I did not care for the idea at all. As our course progressed, I found journal keeping less of a chore and decided that there are some definite advantages . . . Because I was always on the alert for "suitable journal materials" I found myself thinking about different ideas, even when I was not studying them . . . in class. It is a good rehearsal for a written exam . . . an opportunity to express myself through the written word. If a favourite topic of mine is not covered in an exam, I can write about it in my journal. Alright, I will admit it – keeping a journal can be enjoyable.'

Working on projects and dissertations
If you have chosen a subject which has a special project, it will usually be spread over a longer time than most course assignments. Typically you will have months to complete, for example, a GCSE Design or

History project; you will know you have a year to complete a final year degree dissertation or project.

This brings with it special problems of keeping your motivation alive. Often you will have the project in the back of your mind even when you are not doing anything in connection with it. You may find yourself ignoring it or haunted by the worry of it. You may also have a plan to work on your project once you have completed other coursework.

In general it is best to start on the project as early as possible, even if it is in the smallest and simplest of ways.

You can keep your motivation going by:

- being clear about what you are being asked: check the project title; keep the question in mind and check (or double-check) what it means. If you have to decide the title yourself, spend active time getting it clear by talking it out with others. Check that your title is specific enough; that you have enough sources of material for reference and, most of all, that your title is exactly what you want to be working on.

- breaking down the project of dissertation into small parts and tackling them one by one, thus seeing some successful outcomes in a step-by-step manner.

- studying in short but frequent bursts. Do a little – but often. It is not too late to start doing so even if you have postponed starting for some time.

- keeping track of what you are doing. A notebook or journal can help you record your progress. You can mention your difficulties and play around with ideas to overcome them, without having to come up with ultimate 'best' solution.

If you are stuck, talk to your tutor

Use your tutors as fully as possible. Once you have given the topic some thought the tutor is likely to be pleased to discuss uncertainties with you, as long as you are not trying to get the tutor to make decisions for you or do not come to see them too early. Ensure you have given some thought and attention to the topic and have some questions to ask; that type of approach is welcomed by tutors and teachers.

- Using friends and others to help you by (a) not expecting yourself to be able to do everything by yourself and (b) *talking out aloud* about the issues that concern you, coursework you are stuck on and so on. You can pep up your interest in the subject or topic by talking to others and working together on aspects of the assignments.

- Know the question before you start. Do not waste time worrying or using up time on the task that has not been set; know exactly what you have to do. See also **The importance of asking questions** (page 8) and **Analysing the assignment question** (page 10).

- Check the regulations. Know the minimum number of words per piece of coursework. Count the words (easy if you are using a computer) and stick to the limits. If you find you have more words than needed, check with a tutor whether this is likely to be penalised.

Completing the task – the idea of Gestalt

Gestalt is a German word for which the closest translation in English is 'completing the whole'. Once you grasp the idea of it, it can be enormously helpful in removing the day-to-day tension of study.

What it means is that you plan study so that you finish a particular task without leaving a part of it undone. These can be small tasks such as making outline notes on a question, organising a pile of notes or writing a first outline of an introduction to an assignment.

What you are aiming to do is to experience a feeling of completion, a feeling that you have done as much as you are able to do at one attempt. If you have judged it right and completed the gestalt, you can walk away from a study task without feeling anxious or burdened but with a feeling of having properly put the task down – not matter how small it was.

Using Post-its

Post-its are small pieces of paper that have a sticky edge which sticks to other pieces of paper. You can buy them in stationery shops throughout the world. Post-its come in different sizes and can be used for different purposes. Here are the three common sizes and some ideas on how to use Post-its.

2 x 1½ inches
- useful quotes
- a small cross-sectional diagram
- a small spider diagram
- a note to yourself

3 x 3 inches
- noting page numbers
- reminding you of what you want to do with this book or set of notes
- cross referencing, eg 'See Sociology notes too'

5 x 3 inches
- key points you want to ...clude in an assignment
- re-ordered on a sheet of A4 or A3 paper to plan a structure
- memory joggers for revision
- lists of things to do today
- the names/dates/events you want to remember
- separate formulae you want to remember and apply

You can get them in different colours – yellow, green, blue, pink and even white, so you can colour code your work, too.

Using colour codes
You will probably find that you underuse colour to help you find the notes and subjects you are seeking. You can do this more easily by keeping study tasks and subjects in different coloured files such as

- colour-coded sections in a ring binder
- coloured cardboard or plastic wallet envelopes
- see-through plastic envelopes with coloured zip-fasteners
- clear see-through plastic wallets in different tints.

You can also use

- coloured pens to put a clear indication on the top of pages on the same topic.
- stars ★, triangles ▽, squares □ and dots ● in different colours to indicate grouped material. You can buy these stick-on shapes both with wall-planners and from big stationery stores.

Learning about colour from dyslexic students
Among my students are over two hundred dyslexic adults many of whom have transformed their learning with word-processing and printing facilities. From them I have learned the importance of the colour, size and style of print on the screen, and its background colour, to readability.

Students whom I have spoken to have found the most readable combinations to be

Letters	Background
White	Dark Grey
Yellow	Blue
White	Mid-grey/Mid-blue

You do not have to be dyslexic to benefit from this colour awareness.

Most of that we read is black lettering on white background, like this book. Most of what we write in ink is black or blue on a white background. It is not the easiest colour combination to read; for those with certain dyslexic conditions the contrast between black and white appears to make print jump or blur.

Some dyslexic students minimise this reading problem by printing out their work from the computer onto coloured sheets – pale green, blue, grey and yellow. Others use coloured acetate sheets to screen print as they read it in pink, yellow, blue or green hues. A few use specially prepared and purchased colour-tinted spectacles to minimise the difficulties with reading.

I have learned from the experiences of others on this use of colour although I am not dyslexic. As I write my black ink pen is travelling over pale blue paper. Using different colours for writing paper helps me to:

- find some topics more easily in my piles of notes by this colour coding
- break up the uniformity of white sheets of paper to make things readable
- vary my use of blue, yellow, black and white in written notes to ensure I am using the most readable colours
- add Post-its in yellow, white or blue to sheets of other coloured paper to break up the sameness of colour.

Using a photograph album

You can make use of a flip over plastic sleeved photo album for keeping key word cards that you are using for an assignment such as an essay, a talk or a piece of revision. Cards can be arranged in the appropriate sequence to enable you to remember them; they can also be seen clearly and not get mis-ordered or damaged.

By flipping over the cards you can follow the story-line of a talk easily or use question-and-answer cards to enable you clearly to make the links and associations between ideas. They can easily be rearranged if you decide to change the order in which the information is arranged or slipped out and stored elsewhere, with a fresh topic replacing the one you were studying.

KEEP TRACK OF TIME

You can keep track of time in a number of ways. *On a longer time scale* you can monitor the year, the term, the month or the semester (which is increasingly common in higher education).

You can either buy a 12 month year planner, available in an

academic year version as well as a calendar year version, or you can make your own with poster paper or a series of A4 sheets. On them you can mark

- deadlines for submission of assignments
- dates you were given assignments and dates for their completion
- the length of time you have for a particular assignment or project.

Using separate coloured lines to indicate the total number of days or weeks you have available to complete them, you can see at a glance when you have several deadlines occuring around the same time. You will also be able to identify visually the amount of time you have available for any project and spread your energies between them. This is known as a GANNT chart.

On a weekly basis you can fill in a time scale such as that on p 34 to monitor how you actually use time and to spot the most useful and usable times of the week for coursework tasks. There is another version of a weekly time chart usable during revision times on p 55, which divides the week into 21 sessions.

On a daily basis give some thought to trying to spot your best times to tackle the various tasks of study – and the times to relax, play or catch up with chores.

Tracking your time with a time chart
If you have difficulty in making time for study or in finding a balance between revision and other activities, completing this time chart may help you identify the most useful times to tackle various study tasks.

How to use the time chart
- Fill in the spaces in the daily record at the end of each day, indicating what you did in each period of an hour or half-an-hour. Record what you did, not what you intended to do.
- Use highlighting pens to indicate the most frequently usable times for study.
- Draw up a new timetable which indicates your best times for study each week. If you can spot two or three hours on five days a week, you will have the basis of some study time to use each week.

Decide on your best time of day – and your second best
If you know something about when you study most effectively you can choose to concentrate your energies on those tasks which are best tackled at particular times of day.

These are times I can best use for writing, tackling tricky problems,

HOURS	MON	TUES	WED	THURS	FRI	SAT	SUN
a.m. 12-5							
5-6							
6-7							
7-8							
8-9							
9-10							
10-11							
11-12							
p.m.12 -1							
1-2							
2-3							
3-4							
4-5							
5-6							
6-7							
7-8							
8-9							
9-10							
10-11							
11-12							

Note: If you are attending full-time education during the day, you may find it more useful to record half-hour units in the late afternoon and evening, as well as in free time and lunch-times during the day or giving some time to **Brainstorming** ideas to myself (see p 151 for how to use brainstorming with others).

There are some times that I can routinely ignore for study purposes either because of tiredness or because experience tells me they are best spent doing other things – cooking, watching television, going for a walk, making phone calls, listening to music, having a swim, meeting a friend, tackling some chores or giving time to someone who needs it.

In this way I can, with practice, give myself guilt-free, unhaunted time off.

Managing routine tasks

I can jot things down on Post-its, put away paper in the correct file, sort out the materials needed for the next day, check my diary, photocopy a handout, talk to a friend about a particular task over the phone or a cup of coffee, look up a book in the library or re-write a revision or review card.

When you are at school, college or university you don't always have a choice of when to study on particular days. You are often forced into your second or even third choice of time. The same happens when you are a student with family and household responsibilities or are studying part-time with work or other life commitments.

Time savers

- Colour code your notes in plastic or cardboard envelopes so you know where to find them at a glance.
- Put a marker in a book to indicate where you will need to start reading. You can use a bookmark, a card or a Post-it note (which will stick on) for this purpose, writing notes on it to remind you what questions you want to answer or which pages are relevant.
- Make the best use of computers. Type in ideas when you get them, saving them for later retrieval and editing into their right place. Index work for ease of retrieval, listing out tasks and deadlines to remind yourself what to do when.
- Do a little each day on tasks you feel are long-term or difficult to handle. Little and often is the rule and spending 10 minutes for five or six days in a week will soon enable you to see progress on a bigger task like a project or dissertation. You can successfully use very short periods of time for very specific study tasks such as 2, 5, 8, 10, 12, 20, 25, 30 or 40 minutes which can be used for:
  - arranging piles of paper in the correct order
  - jotting down questions you want to use when reading a particular book

- recalling the five key points you have just read by writing them on a card
- drawing a diagram or cross-section
- sketching the first ideas on an assignment
- doing a spider diagram of your first ideas
- calling a friend to check your understanding of a question

and many more such tasks.

Changing time patterns?

If you change your routine, for whatever reason, this pattern may alter in a way that previously unusable times become usable.

If your normal pattern changes during busy periods when you are completing assignments or preparing for an exam then try out a new time for routine tasks or creative ones.

You may also be forced to use routine times for more creative tasks because of pressure. If you have to do so, sometimes you can find yourself in a groove which enables you to be more creative than usual; you may reap the benefit of sustaining focus on a task.

How to meet deadlines

This chapter is filled with ideas for meeting coursework deadlines and in the rest of the book you will find ideas for meeting revision deadlines for exams too. However, there are some guidelines which can be applied to all tasks you face.

Do something early

If you write something down, even if it is only a few ideas on a scrap of paper, you feel as though you have made a start. As long as you are careful to put the piece of paper way in a file or folder where you can find it (see p 26), you will slowly build up what you have to do. So it is an idea to do something immediately you have been given an assignment. This is the principle used in writing this book; I have collected useful ideas in a series of files so that every time I have gone to write something, there is something to start on.

Make an outline

Do some outline plans of what it is you are going to write or design. Allow yourself several tries; do not feel you have to 'get it right' at a first attempt. Freeing yourself up from believing that you have 'got it right' immediately enables you to try out ideas and not be stuck.

Make a rough draft

When you have enough material, try a first very rough draft of your final piece of work. Even in stages, a draft introduction or a draft of the middle section, you will save time and improve the quality of the final version if you get the drafting stage right. You can re-draft your first rough outlines, until you are satisfied.

Use school or college time to the full
You can make a start at many course tasks before you go to your home. By finding some information from a library, working quietly in an empty classroom or by talking to a friend about the task you have to do you can save time you would otherwise spend at home.

USING COMPUTERS TO HELP WITH YOUR COURSEWORK

Schools, colleges and universities are thronging with students who are making excellent use of computers to help them with their studies.

If you have the use of a computer and are attracted to use it for your studies, there are a very wide range of uses you can make of it to tackle coursework and deadlines. You can check out your own use of one in **Using a computer – a checklist** on page 38.

Will you have to use a computer to do your coursework?
How much use you will be able to make of a computer will depend on the amount of time that is available to you; you have a lot more scope to use it fully and creatively if you have your own as opposed to the use of the college or school computer for a few hours a week, in competition with others. The extent to which you are able to use it will depend on the available hardware (the facilities of the computer itself) and the software (the programs you can run on it).

If you are studying in higher education on a higher diploma, degree or post-graduate course, it is becoming increasingly likely that you will develop some familiarity with some aspects of computers during your studies. In particular, many students find the word processing packages invaluable to record their essays, projects, reports and dissertations.

So although you can still in Britain and other countries study for many degree level qualifications without computing skills, submitting handwritten essays or having your work typed up by someone else, it has become the norm that students use word processors. There is little doubt that trend will continue into the twenty-first century.

Further, there are some courses in higher education which are difficult to complete or at least at which you are at a disadvantage without a computer of your own. One obvious example is a Computer or Programming course but in subjects like Electronic Engineering, you are likely to be at a disadvantage in relation to your peers if you're not able to work at a final year project on your own equipment and print the finished document on a good quality ink-jet or laser printer (which is usually available in the university or college).

Using a computer – a checklist

Functions   *Do you/could you use it this way?*
                                     ✓ Yes/?Perhaps/XNo

For keeping a list of resources
As an index of what you have
done so far topic by topic

As a note book to record
thoughts and ideas
see **Starting a learning journal** (pp 27–28)
see **Keep a diary or notebook** (p 50)

As a reminder pad or diary

For typing in the text of an
assignment

As an editor and word processor

To produce graphics and visually
clear printout eg colour graphics

For 'number crunching' (sorting
out an analysing numerical
information you feed it).

Other uses (specify them)

Help is available for using computers

There is a very wide range of specialist help available throughout the education system to enable you to learn the skills you need, whether you are an absolute beginner or well-versed in the use of computers. Computer services in higher education offer one to one advisory interviews, drop in 'problem clinics', training sessions or the use of particular software such as word-processing or spreadsheet packages.

You can also use friends and classmates to help. One group of four mature students spent a Saturday together (with a pub lunch in the middle) and taught themselves a graphics package called Harvard Graphics, so that each of them were able to use it in subsequent assignments. There is expertise around to be tapped amongst your peer group of students.

3
Organising your Revision

WHAT DOES 'REVISION' REALLY MEAN?

Much revision is misnamed as many students find themselves trying to learn and memorise topics for the first time when they start to revise. Although the revise-as-you-go technique described in **Key word revision cards** is an effective way to revise and although most revision begins some weeks before the exam, you can learn these new topics efficiently if you use the appropriate ideas contained in this section of the book; you will find other revision ideas in both Chapter Two and Chapter Four.

Efficient revision
Efficient revision replaces shallow learning with learning in some depth; replaces bewilderment with confidence; replaces the myth of a few fortunate people with photographic memories with the realisation that *you* can use your visual memory to aid recall; and replaces the common – and useless – feeling of guilt with a structured revision programme.

The features of efficient revision are that you:

- set yourself a *clear and specific target*
- *set a time scale* for each task, not 'I must do it', but 'I must do it by X time'
- pick *a task which is sufficiently demanding*, ie that is neither too easy nor too difficult at that moment
- can *verify your success* in learning the topic both to yourself (by testing yourself in some way) or to others (by using them as testers, for example)
- having a *feeling of accomplishment* after completing the task.

Thus features of efficient revision are **Planning your revision,**

Problem checklist

I have/may have problems with	Tick if it applies to you	Brief Tips	Where to find out more (pp)
Getting started with revision		Make a list of what you have got to do subject by subject. Use the system suggested in this book.	39-46
Deciding when I should start revising		Now. It's never too early to start and you can revise until close to the exams.	51-54
Understanding what I am revising		Ask yourself questions about what you are doing: know what you are revising and why.	8-9 63
Leaving my revision too late		Try doing a small piece of revision on a topic that interests you *now* – thirty mins. may be enough. Nibble away at the revision.	29 50-54
Revising by myself		Know what you are doing (see *What should I revise?*) Could you and a friend help each other?	39-46 146-152
Making a revision timetable that works		Have a trial period of a week or two to get it right. Be flexible.	51-54
Knowing the best way to revise		See *How to revise*. It is essential to recall what you have just tried to learn *immediately*.	54-60
How to use my notes and/or books for revision		Use your notes if you know they are good enough. Improve them and reorganise them if they are not.	46-48
The order in which to revise subjects or topics		See *What should I revise?* Vary subjects and topics to keep your interest going.	39-46
Knowing which topics to revise		See *What should I revise?* Know your strengths and weaknesses. Look at old exam papers. Speak to people who can guide you.	8-9 39-46 83-85
Revising mathematics and other number-based subjects		Practise answering questions without books giving you answers. Time yourself for exam length answers.	56-58 80-82
Whether to revise all topics or to ignore some		You can't usually revise all topics equally well. Most people like to cover at least 70%.	39-46
Concentrating		See *How can I improve my concentration?* Make sure you've got a good place to revise.	24-26
Making enough time for revision		Although there is never enough time and you need breaks, time off and relaxation, planning a revision timetable will help.	51-55
Finding a good place to revise		Find a place where you like to be and which has a good feel to it.	25-26 50-51 120-121
Deciding how many hours a day or week to revise		Make a weekly timetable. This can help decide the number of hours you revise. This will vary from 15 to 40 hours a week of private study. Set yourself daily targets.	51-55
Whether to take time off for relaxation and a social life		Take short breaks and at least a day a week and an evening or two off.	23 51-55 109

Organising your revision time, knowing **How to revise** and **Memorising techniques** and each of these is considered in turn.

PLANNING YOUR REVISION

1 *Developing a complete picture* of what you might be examined on in a particular subject will help you decide what to revise and with which topic to begin your revision. Using the suggestions below will prevent this from being overwhelming.

2 You can develop this whole picture by consulting *a syllabus* for the course. If you have, as is quite common, never seen one, your subject teacher is likely to have one and libraries in schools (sometimes) and colleges, polytechnics and universities (usually) keep copies. It may not be necessary to find the syllabus however. Many internal examinations ie exams set and marked within the school or college, are based upon the work you have actually been presented with during the year. Thus, the main topic and sub-topic headings from your notes or handouts from teachers and lecturers can give you quite a complete picture. Questions you have been answering and emphasis given to particular topics can give further guidelines.

It is advisable that you check with teachers and lecturers about the scope of the examination (and use any guidelines you obtain from them).

3 You will find anxiety you feel about 'covering the syllabus' is reduced if you are clear and specific about what you are revising, why you are revising it and how it fits into the overall revision of that subject. One way of deciding this is to *take a separate sheet of paper for each subject* you are studying and write on it the *principal topics* and *sub-topics* that you have studied on the course leading to the examination. For some subjects you may need a second sheet of paper. Arrange the topics and sub-topics in columns, allowing 4 or 6 cm space between each column.

To clarify terminology in the example (p 43) 'Geography' is the subject, 'National Parks' is the topic and 'Homes in National Parks' is a sub-topic.

Working with subjects, topics and symbols

Once you have listed the principal topics and sub-topics for each subject, you can use this simple symbol system to indicate the amount of interest, understanding/knowledge, ease or difficulty, urgency and usefulness of each.

How much
INTEREST
do you have in it?

Very interested
Quite interested
A bit interested
Not interested

How much
*UNDERSTANDING
AND KNOWLEDGE*
do you have of it?

Clearly know/understand it
Know it/understand it quite well
Understand/know a bit but
probably not enough for *pass*
answer standard
Don't know it/understand it at all

How
EASY OR DIFFICULT
do you find it?

Easy to do/understand
Quite easy to do/understand
Quite difficult to understand
Most difficult to understand

How *SOON* is the exam
how much *TIME* do
you have?

Very soon; little time
Soon, some time
Quite soon; a bit more time
Some way off; most time

How *USEFUL* is it?
For example, how likely
is it to come up in the
exam? How useful is it for
other topics or subjects? Can
you use it in your everyday life?

Essential
Useful
Of some use
Of no use

How much
CONFIDENCE
do you have in
tackling this topic?

Very confident
Quite confident
A little confidence
No confidence

How *RELAXED* are
you about this topic?

Very relaxed and composed
Quite composed
A little anxious
Uptight and panicky

How good is
*ACCESS TO
MATERIALS*
you need?

Plenty of materials readily available
Enough available to me
Worryingly little material accessible
Can't find a thing or can't get to it

How much *IMPORTANCE*
is placed upon the topic
or task by you and your
tutors (if there is a
difference – notice it)

IMP.IMP.IMP. Of vital importance
IMP. IMP. Quite a lot of importance placed on it
IMP. Only a little importance
UNIMP. Unimportant

When completing it:

- You don't *have* to use a symbol from each of these five sections above. Thus, if *usefulness* does not seem relevant to a particular topic, then do not write that symbol next to it.

- You can invent your own symbols if you'd prefer; there's nothing magic about these.

Deciding priorities

Using the symbol system can help you decide your priorities. Look in particular for circled symbols, both positive and negative. *Circled positive symbols are a good starting point*, particularly if there are two or more together. This is particularly the case if you are finding it difficult to get started on your revision or your concentration has been poor. It will help your confidence to tackle a topic at which there is a high probability you will succeed. The second most positive symbol also represents topics that you are likely to be able to revise competently at an early stage.

You are probably going to find it more difficult to learn and immediately recall those *circled negative symbols*, particularly if you only have a short time left in which to revise.

What should I revise and in what order?

Example

Kate, aged 15, has listed some principal topics on her 4th Year Geography syllabus. Next to each topic she has written symbols to reflect her *interest, understanding/knowledge* and the *ease or difficulty* she finds in each. Later she describes how she uses it to decide what to revise and in what order.

- You can mix in some topics with the more negative symbols in between those topics with more positive symbols, as your revision progresses and your confidence grows.

- Some people like to tackle some difficult topic first. They may feel by doing so that they have set themselves a positive challenge or challenged their fear. There is no correct order. Choose the order that meets your needs.

In the example, Kate said

'I will start by revising the work which I found most difficult and the work which I did earlier in the course. I will do this because when I sit down

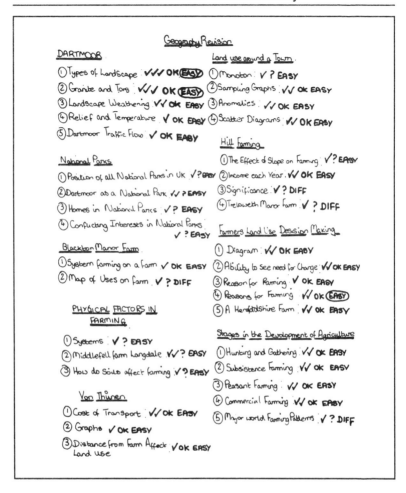

ready to revise I am at my most alert and my concentration is good.

'By looking at the list I made for revising, I will mix in early topics I did, eg 'Types of Landscape', 'Granite Tors', with topics which I found difficult, eg 'Significance of Hill Farming' and 'Major world farming patterns'.

'I will revise last the subjects I found easy, eg 'Reasons for Farming' and those that are fresh in my mind, eg 'Hunting and Gathering', 'Subsistence Farming'. I already understand these quite well and they will not take long to learn when I come to finishing off my revision.'

Kate's choice of order for topic revision feels correct to her. It is a subject in which she has a fair degree of confidence: a fact reflected by the large number of positive symbols on the page. This confidence enables her to start her revision with some relatively difficult topics. If the page had been covered with negative symbols, it would probably have been the best confidence-building plan to start with a few positive symbols.

Encouraging revision of difficult topics

Colin Richman devised this system to revise for pharmacy degree final exams and gave this report on how it was progressing with about four weeks to go to the exams:

'In an attempt to cover the topics I had rather not, I used a system of ticks. An example – under Pharmaceutical Chemistry (Pharm Chem) I have covered the topics of:

1. Enzyme inhibitors
2. Anticancer drugs
3. Anti-inflammatory drugs
4. Optical isomerism
5. Anti-AIDS therapy
6. Prodrugs
7. Drug stability and interactions
8. Isoteric modification

Firstly I cover the subject I enjoy, and have a personal interest in, ticking them off as I go with my '*colour tick system*':

Red tick   =   Read
Green tick = Revision notes made (in glorious Technicolor)
Blue tick =   Reread and flashcard written
Black tick = Exam question covered.

So the game is to read and make notes on the subjects in between and JOIN THE TICKS!! The contest is between Pharm Chem and the other four disciplines, to see which one will have the largest amount of continuous ticks.

(So far Pharmacognosy is leading with 7, then Pharm Chem and Pharmacology 5 each, then with Pharm Chem in a strong tactical position!!!)'

Spotting examination questions

Question spotting is a risky business. Given that an examiner could ask many different questions about a particular topic, trying to guess a particular question is obviously difficult. In many subjects a core of topics are going to appear, with some variation from year to year, eg a topic appearing in three or four years for a five year period. In some examination papers there is some reasonably sure 'banker' question. Examinations which are set and marked *internally* ie within the school or college, are going to concentrate on the actual topics which the teacher or lecturer has presented to groups during the course. It is likely that *topic spotting* is more reliable in these exams, whereas in *externally* set and marked examinations, eg most GCSE and Advanced level subjects, the emphasis of the questions will be to reflect the work of many students and their teachers. Different emphasis is likely to be given to topics in separate schools and colleges. GCSE includes internal and external assessment.

There is no substitute for extra work if you want to be certain of being able to answer the number of questions required. One effective way of preparing is to **Devise questions around a topic**, another to **List useful definitions**. The overall strategy is laid out in the flow diagram on p 47.

Devise questions around a topic

By practising asking questions about a particular topic you can increase your flexibility and preparedness for the examination itself. *List* past exam questions, grouping them into *types* of question and according to *emphasis* they may have in common. Add to these any questions you have been asked during your course and any that you and others could make up to give other angles on the topic. Check to see which questions occur most frequently on past papers, as one rough guide to the likelihood of particular questions occurring.

List useful definitions

Make lists of definitions of the *key words, ideas or concepts* that you may need to use in the examination. Learn these as part of your revision. The following ideas can help you plan your revision.

Build up good notes from which to revise

Organise and, if necessary, reorganise your notes by:

- Keeping all your notes, essays, reports and other material on a particular *topic* together. As the studying year proceeds it is often unnecessary for material to be separated because of the date you completed it or the type of material.
- Grouping related topics together for ease of revision: related topics can be revised together.
- Discussing your notes with others. Criticise them and, where appropriate, re-write parts of them.

- Reducing your bulky notes to key words and key ideas as explained in **Key word revision cards**. Use these cards for the major part of your revision, cross referencing them with your original notes.
- Drawing together brief summaries of topics and sub-topics in a visually creative way. One method is to use simple *spider diagrams* to help you remember the main points of a topic. Each leg of the spider can be a different colour to help you differentiate between them associating a colour and a piece of information. The number of legs your spider possesses will vary! These can be easily and quickly reproduced at the beginning of an exam.

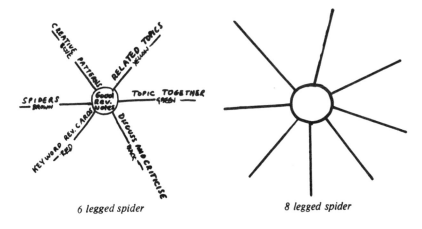

6 legged spider   *8 legged spider*

Patterned notes

Patterned notes are another way of summarising your understanding and finding links and associations between information and ideas.

Usually when students make notes they try to force their ideas into a linear (straight line) structure, eg:

(1) Related topics
(2) Discuss and criticise
(3) Key word revision cards

This often creates problems when they think of a new idea that does not fit into the structure. Alternatively, dissatisfaction with the order of the items, or remembering another item and having no space in which to add it can lead to several re-writes and re-orderings.

Patterned notes help to overcome this problem. They can be used creatively to allow the mind to associate freely (they are sometimes called **creative brain patterns** or **mind maps**). They can also be used for summarising very quickly what you have just been revising. In 5 minutes, using this system, you can recall a complete topic on paper or card.

You start patterned notes in the centre of a sheet of paper. Your subsequent ideas can splay out around it. When you are using it creatively, don't attempt to evaluate your ideas, just write them down. When all your thoughts on the topic are down on paper then you can evaluate the ideas and decide which order you will put them in. By this method you are trying to separate the creative and evaluative processes of the mind. You can use colours to group information and ideas together and add numbers to indicate which ideas are most important or the order in which you would answer a question. Make your notes as brief as possible. They are just for you and don't have to make sense to anyone else.

Some best times to use patterned notes are: when you are about to start writing a piece of work, eg as an outline answer to a question in the examination; when you want to check your recall of the topic you have just revised; when you want to summarise some longer notes; in planning an essay or the answer to any coursework question; as a facing or front page to your more conventional notes, ie you can use the two forms of notes alongside each other. Experiment and find out when you find them most useful. More information about this approach can be found in Tony Buzan's book *Use Your Head*.

This is an example of a mind map to check whether you are ready to study:

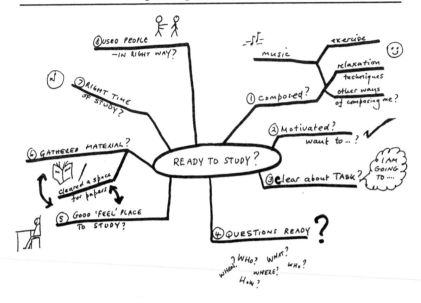

ORGANISING YOUR REVISION TIME

Have an overview of what you have to revise

Deciding what to revise offers suggestions on how to do this.

This will help you decide how much to revise and in what order. How much of a subject to revise is a difficult issue. For the majority of examinations you can be very successful without attempting to revise 100% of the syllabus. There are some examinations for some professional groups that demand very high levels of perfect knowledge about certain key areas, eg for doctors, accountants and lawyers. The majority of examinations and examiners do not expect the whole syllabus to be 'covered'. Obviously, the more you cover in your revision the more chances you have of finding questions you can answer. However, this will still depend on how carefully you have checked with your teachers, syllabus and examinations and which topics you have revised, eg it would be possible to miss a topic which is compulsory and worth more marks than other topics. **Know your examinations** and you will maximise the chances of your finding questions you can answer.

My guess – and it is only a guess, with the provisos mentioned already – is that covering 70% of a typical syllabus during revision would provide a good chance of finding enough questions to answer. As I consider this to be the least reliable guideline in this book, I would strongly recommend you seek the guidance of others, teachers and lecturers for each subject you take if you are concerned about this issue.

Keep a diary or notebook

There are several uses for these.

- You can use this to monitor your progress, commenting on how well you are progressing and noting points of which you wish to be reminded.
- To note down ideas and information as they occur. These can be transferred later to revision cards or notes.
- To plan the next day's work on the evening before.
- To keep by the side of your bed to note down good ideas, clear thoughts, information or even dreams that you have remembered. You can use it if you wake at night or first thing in the morning when you wake.

You may find other uses for them. You may also wish to carry blank postcards around with you for noting down the same sort of information, as an alternative or in addition to a diary or notebook.

Vary subjects, topics and methods throughout your revision

Vary these each week and each day. You will find that you are more likely to sustain your concentration by doing so. At the same time, mix the difficulty of the topics revised, using the confidence gained from one piece of work successfully completed to help you tackle a slightly more difficult topic.

Where to revise

There is a Checklist of questions about your best study environment on pp 25-26; here are some key tips for the revision period.

(1) The key feature of where to revise is that you seek for yourself a place where you like to be and where it is easiest to work. It must have a good feel to it: a kitchen table (where I am writing now); lying on your bed; at a desk, in an armchair, can all have this feel.

(2) It is advisable to work some of the time at a desk, to prepare yourself for exam conditions, particularly closer to the exams.

(3) A clear desk or table top, with enough space to have materials assembled and accessible around you. This will reduce time wasting and delaying tactics!

(4) Your area of a room should be well lit (a table lamp may help), well ventilated and warm enough to be comfortable without

causing you to feel drowsy. It should also ensure you have the minimum unwanted interruptions and distractions.

(5) A pleasant, non-distracting view can aid concentration. As I write I have a wall in front of me. It is light coloured and I can see two pictures I like and a chart on which I am ticking off my progress in writing this book. Soon I will be ticking off **Where to revise**. A pin board or wall chart in front of you can be very useful to plan and record your progress.

(6) There is a lot of debate and argument in homes about whether you need to be working in a quiet environment. I don't believe there is one answer to this issue. If you, as the student, feel the need for quiet then it is important. If, on the other hand, listening to the radio, tapes or records aids your work, then continue to do so.

Television is another dimension, for the visual image is powerful and watching television requires the use of two major senses. I can only listen to television when I am working, not watch and listen. Both can be used to advantage, by helping you relax and/or associating some sound or vision with a particular revision topic.

The essential point is to be honest with yourself. Is the environment you've created really helping your study – or acting, to some degree at least, as a substitute for work?

13 ideas for organising your time

Here are 13 ideas to help you organise time.

1. *Make a revision timetable* going day-by-day from now until the examinations begin and for the period between examinations. The problem with revision timetables is that they often go wrong after the first day: to counteract this:

   — Have a two week or one week trial period to enable you to determine what tasks you can realistically complete in a day.
   — Be flexible, eg different subject headings for each day will enable you to vary the topics you revise.

   An example of a revision timetable is included.

2. *Pin up your timetable* or time plan on a wall in a prominent place eg above your table or desk. Coloured pens can make it clear and attractive.

3. *Revise as you go:* start weeks before the exams. If you haven't started before reading this, start now. It's never too early to start and you can still revise until very close to your examinations. Starting 6 to 8 weeks before the exam is a typical revision period for most students.

4. *Include in your revision* timetable any unfinished work you still have to do as part of your year's studies. You do not have to complete this work *before* starting revision. You can revise this subject work as soon as it is completed, so it can become part of your revision.

5. *Know how you use the 168 hours in the week.* You can use the **Time Chart** to calculate exactly how you have used the time in one week and record hours in these categories, below. Alternatively, you can do a rough calculation and complete the table below. You have been provided with a daily and weekly column; complete either or both according to which you find easier.

TIME CHART	Total hours	
	Daily	Weekly
Sleeping, dressing, washing, etc	_____	_____
Travel	_____	_____
Classes, laboratories, etc.	_____	_____
Going out socially	_____	_____
Recreation and exercise	_____	_____
Watching television	_____	_____
Eating	_____	_____
Domestic responsibilities and tasks	_____	_____
Totals	_____	_____
Hours remaining in the day/week that may be used for private study	_____	_____
	(Total subtracted from 24 hrs.)	(Total subtracted from 168 hrs.)

6. *Set yourself a daily target of revision hours.* An alternative to a large scale or weekly revision timetable is to set yourself a daily target of revision hours eg 4 hours a day. This time unit can be shown on a chart marked off in quarter hour units with your favourite colours, to show you effective and concentrated use of time. You could use this idea by itself or alongside marking off topics you have revised on a chart.

Angela, a final year undergraduate, combined this with positive self statements ('It's really working', 'I've 40 whole days left') to successfully complete her revision. She monitored the quarter hour units on a chart and felt a sense of achievement and optimism: there are a great many quarter hours in 4 hours revision a day for 40 days!

7. *Working late at night*. As explained in **Getting to sleep at night** there are wide differences in people's ability to work effectively late at night or the early hours of the morning. For a typical student 3 or 4 hours work in an evening is likely to be as much as they can effectively tackle. It would certainly not be advisable to work very late or long the night before an exam. On other nights, developing the effective self-monitoring this book is encouraging, will enable you to decide whether you are working efficiently.

8. *For routine revision*, you can *work in short periods of time* ie as short as 20-30 mins. Some topics and subjects call for longer periods but numerous sub-topics can be revised in this way. Mathematical, Scientific or problem based revision will often require longer periods eg 1 hour, to follow through a sequence of techniques and knowledge.

9. It is important to *set a time limit on completing a task*, ie 'I will do X by . . . '

10. *Reward yourself* by taking *breaks* of at least a few minutes between work spells. You can take longer breaks for a drink or to watch a favourite TV programme. Breaks can also be used for actively recalling what you have just been trying to learn.

11. *Divide the week into 21 sessions*. Another way of organising your time is to see the week as seven mornings, seven afternoons and seven evenings. Think of each session as a maximum of 3 hours long. Plan to work, formally in school or college or privately, around 15 sessions, giving a maximum working week of 45 hours, out of the 168 hours in the week. Using this system, ensure you take about 6 sessions for relaxation, entertainment and as a complete break from study.

12. *The number of hours a week to revise* will vary widely according to what level of examinations you are studying, how many subjects you are taking and the amount of formal study, eg classes, lectures you are continuing to attend. However, private revising time close to the examinations is likely to be a minimum of 15 hours a week and a maximum of around 40 hours a week.

13. *A very important rule of thumb*. For every one unit of time, eg half

an hour you give to reading ie trying to take in or assimilate information you should spend at least the same amount of time on trying to recall what you have just read.

It is by recalling that we remember what we have read (heard or seen). So, the order is:

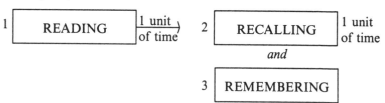

1 | READING | 1 unit of time →   2 | RECALLING | 1 unit of time

and

3 | REMEMBERING

'It really works!'

Katherine Turner used this approach in the summer term before her GCSEs. She writes:

'My greatest problem in the past has been organizing a successful work timetable – until! – I discovered your idea of dividing the day into 3 sessions, am, pm and evening. It REALLY WORKS! I have used it to plan all the work I have had this half-term.'

HOW TO REVISE

In order to revise efficiently, you can draw upon a wide range of ideas about how we learn. These have been grouped together in Chapter Four **Improving Your Memory** and are relevant to all subjects at whatever level. Additionally, specific ideas are included to help those studying Mathematically based subjects, Science and Technology. These are preceded by a description of a reliable **Basic revision method** and the suggestion of **Using key word revision cards** system.

Q. What is the commonest revision fault?
A. The commonest revision fault is to sit passively with book or notes open in front of you for hours, attempting to read and 'take it all in'. Frequently, the results are poor; you do not remember most of what you were reading; long periods are spent over the same page whilst feeling increasingly disheartened.

Q. What method can you use to correct the fault?
A. This basic revision method uses a number of different learning ideas in combination. It is very active; it involves repetition and testing yourself; it ensures you minimise mistakes; it involves using your visual and aural memory; it breaks down learning into manageable parts and ensures you are recalling recent learning. (Continued on p. 56.)

A time chart

The first week of this timetable is complete in some detail: other weeks can be completed in the same way. If you are continuing to attend full time education during the day, the evenings or weekends will become more important and can be sub-divided into smaller units, if necessary.

DAYS OF THE MONTH OF:	MON	TUES	WED	THURS	FRI	SAT	SUN
(Month)	7	8	9	10	11	12	13
a.m.	Subject A	subject C	voluntary work	Subject D	WHOLE DAY	Subject E	Subject E
p.m.	walk Squash Coffee-friend	Shopping	Subjects B and C	Subjects B and C	VISIT TO	Review of ABCD	TV Friend's home
Evening	Subject B (2 topics)	Subject A (1 topic)	Subject C	Subject B	TOWN	Meet friend at DISCO	Review cards Plan next week
	14	15	16	17	18	19	20
a.m.							
p.m.							
Evening							
	21	22	23	24	25	26	27
a.m.							
p.m.							
Evening							
	28	29	30	31	1	2	3
a.m.							
p.m.							
Evening							
	4	5	6	7	8	9	10
a.m.							
p.m.							
Evening							

Time already committed during the Examination and Revision period e.g. social events, classes, exams.

Time that may be available for revision: you would fill in subjects or topics in these spaces.

If it is coupled with the **Key word revision cards** idea, you add to these concise, manageable summaries; colour and design to stimulate visual memory and frequent use in very short bursts of time to ensure continued recall and memory.

A basic revision method

This is a basic method for most routine descriptive (word based) revision and some problem solving, mathematical revision, involving either four or five steps.

Step one
Read your notes and seek answers to questions, as described in **The importance of asking questions** (pp 8-11).

Be as active in your reading as possible eg talk to yourself, walk around the room (even though people may give you funny looks). Speak into a tape recorder.

Step two
When you feel you have understood and can remember what you have read, close up your notes.

Step three
Now actively recall what you've just been reading, asking again the same questions without looking at your notes, until you have exhausted your recall of the whole topic you've been revising. Whilst doing so write down what you have recalled in brief notes on a card or a sheet of paper. It may help you to have the question written down to refer to in the recalling process.

Step four
Check the original notes with the new ones. Have you recalled all the answers to the questions you were asking?

If yes, you have created a *master card*, which you can use to re-revise without having to consult the original lengthier notes. *If no,*

Step five
Re-read your original notes as in Step one above, looking particularly for those points you originally missed. Repeat Steps two to four above, writing out all the points again, not just those missed the first time: by doing so, you will still be treating the topic as a whole and improving your recall on the whole topic.

This may appear time consuming and cumbersome but it is not. It ensures a high degree of recall which reading a lot of notes does not do.

Using key word revision cards

Key word revision cards are a popular and effective way of developing your revision notes. The object is to write (or draw) brief outline notes immediately after you have completed work on a topic. Your intention is to record the minimum number of words to retain a full understanding of the information the next time you look at, and use, the card. These words – the *key* words, are designed to stimulate your recall of the topic without the necessity to write complete sentences or continuous prose. Cards can also be used for recording, and recalling, diagrammatic data, cross-sectional drawings, graphs, tables or formula.

Starting your cards

You can start making these cards at any time, not just at those times, closer to exams, which you think of as revision times. Immediately you have completed a piece of homework or coursework you could summarise it onto a card, which as well as being a preparation for revision will become a part of revision. If you read an interesting article, see a relevant television programme or find a useful section in a book, brief outline notes on a card can quickly capture the moment.

The cards will quickly build up and can be grouped in subject/topic groups. They can be kept in boxes, plastic wallets and/or be held together with elastic bands.

Cards can be of any size. The three most popular sizes are A5, postcard size and a size somewhat smaller than postcard size. Postcard size tends to be the most popular as you can condense a considerable amount of information on to it and it is very convenient to carry in pocket or bag. Cards have advantages over paper in that they are more durable. A further advantage is that they help you develop confidence in your ability to manage the volume of revision you are required to tackle. Revising from a series of small, non-bulky cards seems so much more manageable than overwhelming piles of A4 notes in files or ring binders. You can always consult your main notes if a point on your card is unclear, amending your cards as you do so. Cards are easy to read on a bus; in a common room; waiting in a corridor or during a lunch-time or break from classes.

Advantages of using your own cards
There is nothing new about a card system like this. Commercially produced cards on particular subjects have become a growth industry over the last decade or two, eg 'Key Facts' cards and their rivals.

Making your own can produce better notes for revision. This is because you can:

- Make them reflect your own understanding and knowledge; highly personal to you.

- Use space in a varied, interesting and more visually recallable way. Each card can be unique, making it very much easier to recall the information.

- You can use colour, boxes and underlining together with graphics, cartoons or diagrams to add vividness to each card. You could use a standardised colour system for your notes: black for information, blue for cross referencing your own thoughts; green for headings; red for key names, dates, book titles. You can train yourself to recall both what you wrote and where it was located on the card. Associating the two will aid your recall of the card.

Some of the other useful aids are included in the outline of a revision card, below. Two completed cards, although reproduced without colour, give some idea of how to construct them.

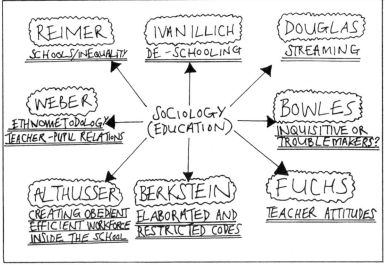

Using abbreviations

Three basic rules in using abbreviations

(1) Be consistent in your use of your own abbreviations. Find a system and a set of standard abbreviations and stick to it.

(2) Do not use abbreviations in work designed to be read by others, eg examiners. The exceptions to this are relatively few (eg, ie, et al, viz are most common).

(3) Keep a note of your own common abbreviations, either in a notebook, on a card or at the front of your file.

In addition, you can devise your own abbreviations for the common terms used in the subjects you study. These would include:

— The subjects themselves eg G = Geography; M.S. = Materials Science.
— The names of professions eg Scs = Scientists; Ecs = Economists; Hs = Historians.
— Concepts, ideas, principles, common practices eg c.w. = casework; Cht. = Chartism; strat. = stratification.

You can also abbreviate by:

— Leaving out unnecessary words thus leaving only the key words you need to retain an understanding of what you have written, eg a, the. Shortening the ends of words eg —ing becomes g.
— Leaving out syllables, eg transport becomes t'port.
— Using foreshortened versions of words you use frequently, eg cd = could; wd = would; shd = should; w/o = without.

This foreshortening is often achieved by leaving out vowels (aeiou). However, it is worth restating that you have to be consistent and use the abbreviations only one way, eg w/o = without in your abbreviation not 'won over' as it does in competitive sport.

Standard abbreviations

Some of the most common and useful abbreviations you can use in note taking and key word revision cards.

p	= page	=	= equals, is the same as
pp/ps	= pages	≠	= does not equal, is different from
f	= following page		
ff	= following pages	<	= less than
ib, ibid	= ibidem = in the same book, chapter, passage, notes	>	= greater than
		∴	= therefore
e.g.	= exampli gratia = for example	∵	= because
op cit	= opere citato = in the work quoted	no.	= number
		qv.	= see
et al	= et alia = and others	~	= about
viz	= videlicet = namely	→	= it follows
i.e.	= id est = that is	alt	= alternative
cf	= confero = compare	fr	= from
c	= circa = about, approximately	exc	= except
v/vs	= versus = against	incl	= including
inf	= infra = below	opp	= opposite
NB	= nota bene = note well	neg	= negative
ref	= with reference to	pos	= positive
esp	= especially	usu	= usually

4
Improving Your Memory

WHAT YOU WILL FIND IN THIS CHAPTER

In the United States of America, the 1990s have been declared the decade of research into the brain. It is clear that we are beginning to learn more about how the brain works, how we learn and remember and this chapter brings you some of those understandings and many practical ideas for improving your memory which are drawn from them.

Here you will find ideas about how we can make the use of both our left and right sides of the brain. Many students are being asked to engage in a number of left-brained tasks such as trying to be objective, rational, logical, theoretical and analytical in both writing and speech. This chapter is full of ideas for tackling these tasks by making the fullest use of your senses and thus bringing into use your right-brain characteristics such as the ability to visualise, be intuitive, draw ideas together and make patterns to help you with some of the left-brain dominated tasks.

You will also find ideas about the use of your eyes and your use of language in improving memory drawn from the field called NLP (neuro-linguistic programming).

You will find ideas for the active use of your senses in different combinations to enhance your memory and some ways of checking your preference for the use of your senses.

The good news is that, whatever your age your memory can be improved. To work well, your memory needs to be used often, be given its exercise, as it were. As you go through these memory ideas, pick out the ones you would like to try and notice the approaches you use most often. Try out different approaches until you find those that suit you. You can do this by seeing if they help you remember some items on a shopping list or some phone numbers as well as using them to recall something you are revising.

Problem Checklist

I have/may have problems with	Tick if it applies to you	Brief tips	Where to find out more (page)
Improving my short-term memory		Try not to take in more than two or three pieces of information at most, at one time. Find links to what you already know.	29,54 63-65 70
Remembering formulae and mathematics		Do lots of worked examples tracing back to clear understandings. Use colour coding for formula, adding visually absurd images to help recall.	80-82
Recalling the detail in diagrams and graphs		Use highly visual active technique, testing yourself on sections of the diagram. Use upward eye movements to visual recall.	75-77 139-143
Not remembering unless you revise close to the exams		Start immediately to make up brief question and answer cards (each unique and varied). Test yourself on the topic and do so again regularly for a few minutes. You will recall them.	8-11 46 57-59
Remembering what I have already revised		Review your key word cards or notes in short bursts at regular intervals by testing yourself.	57-59 150
No matter how hard you try you cannot remember what you want to remember		You are trying too hard – 'trying' is not a good idea; doing practical multi-sensory active things is a good idea.	67-77
How to remember dates and names		Big bold colourful drawings and images linking dates, events and people together.	71-72
Remembering facts		Pay full attention to the material in a relaxed frame of mind. Use your senses to the full to find links with the facts.	69-77
Your mind going blank when you know you know it		Understand how your eye movements affect recall; use it to help you unblock the memory. Start writing and doing something; learn some calming techniques.	75-77
Forgetting what you learned last week		Regularly review the topic at intervals suggested. Make sure you paid full attention to the topic by means of active techniques like Question and Answer.	8-11 46

WAYS OF REMEMBERING

The best way of remembering is to have a real understanding of a topic which has been achieved by finding the right questions to ask and seeking answers to them. In this way, you come to see the connections between things; how A links with B, B with C and so on.

Such understanding can be developed by some of the ideas that follow, which will aid your recall of information.

Association
Words, numbers or pictures take meaning in relation to the information around them. It is these links with the information around them which fundamentally affects their meaning.

A simple example would be the word LOVE. Its meaning and context changes with the words around it. LOVE, Forty; the LOVE bug; I LOVE you, God of LOVE – all conjure up very different perspectives.

Where these links – these associations – form in chains, you may find that a real and lasting understanding develops. Even if this fails to happen, association techniques, both visual and verbal, can aid your memory very effectively.

Group objects to form associations and links
Grouping items together and forming links and associations between them in your mind. You could practise this idea by the tray exercise, a well known game played at parties. The object is to remember items on a tray, by associating one with another in practical ways, eg scissors cutting string and paper; pens writing on paper; pens kept in a jar. You can find these kinds of associations with objects located next to each other.

Repetition
Write out things several times. This can help with spelling words, learning tables, learning definitions and dates when events occurred.

Repeat aloud several times. Do this to learn tables, quotations, poems and other extracts from literature.

Listen several times to a record or tape. Read into the tape recorder and replay it to yourself several times. Listen to it as you fall asleep at night.

Re-read information several times. By itself this is not as effective when coupled with a questioning and/or association technique.

Testing yourself
A basic revision method, Key word revision cards and **Time and recall**

(page 65) demonstrate the importance of testing yourself in memorising.

Wherever possible, learn topics in a logical whole unit, looking for the natural breaks between topics. Where the whole topic feels too much to revise as one unit, break it down into logical sub-topics or parts.

Don't learn all the parts separately and then test yourself. Build up your learning by revising the first part and testing yourself on it before revising the second. Test yourself on the first two parts before moving on to the third part and so on.

Finally, you are likely to recall most readily:
– The facts you learn first (Primacy).
– The things you work at most frequently (Frequency).
– The topics you have studied most recently (Recency).
– Topics you worked at with maximum concentration and intensity.

Forming a link to places
Create a picture in your imagination to which you link facts. This can be real or imaginary. If you use a real scene you could imagine your room, the kitchen, your street or other familiar places, associating particular facts with particular objects. You can have several different places and associate a topic with each.

You would also use a technique the Romans and Greeks used for remembering. They imagined themselves walking through a palace and pausing at particular doors, stairways or passages associating them with particular objects.

You can do the same in your own home by:

• placing a particular topic you wish to remember in a particular location
• keeping your study of particular subjects or particular topics to a particular room or chair, using your senses to the full to enable you to fully experience studying that topic in that place and time
• keeping your notes and books for particular subjects or topics in their specified area of your home; thus when you picture that place you access memory of that subject
• placing an item you wish to recall in a distinct and entirely new environment and associating it with that unique place.

KEY STEPS TO A BETTER MEMORY

1   Use it regularly. The more you give your memory to do, using appropriate approaches for you, the better it will function.

2 If you want to remember something then find a clear link with something about which you already know or have some knowledge or understanding. Draw upon past experiences to make links with the new information.

3 Be positive. Believe you can learn and remember it. Set out to enjoy learning and to find the most sensory useful as well as enjoyable techniques that suit you.

4 Remember pictures. Most people underuse their visual memory. For example, if you are trying to remember an address, make pictures of the street and imagine walking down it, pausing to look at the road sign and the colour of the door, with the number on it. If you do not know the place invent a picture to go with the address 18 Ford Road.

5 Use all your senses to make a picture. Hear, smell, touch, taste as well as see the object – or at least use as many of these senses as is realistic.

6 Understand your own best memory triggers. Use this chapter to identify your own best remembering techniques.

7 Build up your memory little by little, linking each 'nibble' of learning with things you already have experienced and can understand.

8 Most importantly, review the new information regularly, actively recalling the last item you learned. Do so at regular intervals.

Some useful review patterns
Time and recall
Here are four examples of the principle of regularly reviewing what you have learned as a fundamental tool of improving memory. It does not matter which you choose. Try to find one that works for you.

Example A
1 Review or revise for one hour.
2 Take a break, 10 minutes later, review for another 10 minutes the key points in any notes *or* write down what you can remember in key notes.
3 The next day review these notes for 5 minutes.
4 Review again in about a month for another 10 minutes. (You may

be unsure you will remember the notes for that long – although you have a very good chance of doing so. In which case build in a check after one or two weeks).

Example B

Revise	1	For up to one hour
Review	2	Later that day
	3	The next day for 2–3 minutes
	4	The next week
	5	The next month
	6	Six months later

Example C

Revise	1	For up to an hour
Review	2	Immediately afterwards
	3	The next day for ten minutes
	4	Two or three days later
	5	Two weeks later
	6	Three months later
	7	Every six months afterwards.

Example D

Revise	1	For up to one hour
Review	2	After one hour
	3	The next day
	4	The next week
	5	The next month
	6	After six months.

These review periods need only be very short – 2 to 10 minutes. Whichever system you use it is the process of re-reviewing that is important.

The four step recall system

When asked to recall the events that occurred at the scene of a crime, the eye witnesses often told remarkably different versions of events. An Open University programme looked at how psychologists had helped the police develop a more effective step recall process.

1. Recall the context

Include in this where you were, what was happening, who was there, what time of day it was, what the weather was like and how you felt.

2. Seek out all that can be remembered including minor details
however apparently irrelevant they may seem. Thus you might describe
the rain on a windscreen, a piece of paper blowing in the wind, the look
on the shopkeeper's face, a blue pram and so on.

3. Question specific parts of the event
Ask yourself for detailed recall of the sequence of events and the most
detailed look at the colour, sound and smells in the situation including
how you felt. For example, what drew your attention to the crime
initially, what happened next and immediately afterwards and so on.

4. Imagine you are seeing it from a different viewpoint
That is, as if you were someone else in the situation or standing
somewhere else and observing what was going on. Example would be
what if you had been the taxi driver, what might you have seen?

However memory can be:
- *selective* — you miss things out and include others in
- *reconstructed* — you can put it together afterwards, perhaps in a
  slightly different order
- *contaminable* — you can be influenced by subsequent events and
  distort images, places, faces.

That is why the vivid techniques of using your senses to the full
association and reviewing are such powerful tools for your learning
and minimise the chance of error occurring. Could you also find an
association between the four step approach above and your revision?

Don't 'try to remember'
'Try to remember' is a phrase I remember from childhood when I had
lost something or had a test. It is still a phrase that I associate with
someone trying to help me find something I have mislaid. I get anxious
to some degree when I hear the words and that I may actually TRY to
remember something. The attempt usually fails because I am too aware
of the process of trying to remember; the word 'try' does not help.

The process that works best is pleasurable and where you have no
awareness of 'trying'. If you attend fully to the topic, question or task
you are focused upon and then recall it – you will be checking that you
have *assimilated* it, ie remembered it.

USING YOUR BRAIN: RIGHT AND LEFT HALVES

One of the firm impressions gained from meeting many thousands of learners is that most of us vastly underuse the capacity of our brain. Understanding the way it works – and in particular, the function of the right and left halves of the brain, can provide a stepping stone to making the best use of your brain.

The left and right halves of the brain process information in somewhat different ways. The right brain responds to art, music and patterns, processing information holistically, grasps the whole picture quickly and is more sensitive to subconscious influences. The left brain tends to work on a step-by-step basis. Most teaching is geared to the left brain.

However, the belief among many researchers into learning is that if you fully involve the right brain with the left brain – enable yourself to call on both, then you vastly increase your ability to use your brain. Making connections and associations between the functions of both halves of the brain enables you to learn and remember vast amounts of information.

Functions of the brain – both left and right

Left-side of brain

words
logic
linear sequence
analysis
number
lists

Right-side of brain

colour
spatial relationship
awareness of space, eg depth
distance, dimension
imagination
dream images
pattern
Gestalt (whole) see p 30

What are you better at?

If you are more on this *left-side* you are more likely to be better at:
If you are more on this *right-side* you are more likely to be better at:

Writing	Drawing
Recognising digits, number and combinations	Verbal material, spoken or written; where you can use or see pictures
Recognising and recalling words	Using photographs and diagrams

Drawing on previously acquired, organised information	Drawing on many patterns, which come in no clear sequence but connect with images you feel
Slower, step-by-step, analysing and detecting	Faster and wide ranging matching up of ideas and images
Spotting differences in sound and language	Spotting differences in touch and 'feel'

USING ALL YOUR SENSES

This is a diagrammatic representation of some ways in which our senses connect.

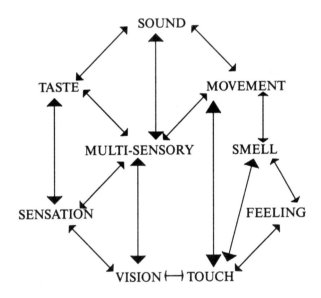

As the arrows in the diagram indicate, you can make links, connections and associations between the senses to help the fullness of your memory of the initial piece of information you set out to learn. There are a number of ideas and examples of how to make these links in the sections that follow.

Make specific links

You can make these multi-sensory associations more specific by linking them

with numbers
with rhythms as in Buzan's number/rhyme system (p 79)
with letters
with places
with people
with colours
and with smells.

What words do you choose most often?

The words you speak can help you detect how you will most effectively learn, remember and recall a piece of information.

Over the course of a few days, notice if you use some of these words more often than others. Ask a friend or family member if they recognise your use of particular words.

visual words   *auditory/sound words*   *sensation/kinaesthetic words*

Tick off ✓ and count up the number of times you use particular words or phrases like these:

picture	hear	touch
clear	say	(I was) thrown
focus	ask	struggle (to remember)
see	note	hit
outlook	tune (in)	irritate
vision	voice	rub (up the wrong way)
spectacle	(strike a) chord	run (with it)
lazy	tone	(put your) finger (on it)
show	(a) ring (to it)	tangible
illustrate	harmony	move
reveal	sound	impress
paint	sing	grope (for a word)

If you find yourself using words from one column a lot more than another then it can help you choose which methods to use when you are learning anything at all – either visual methods, auditory methods or active kinaesthetic methods.

You will often kind it is a combination of two of these, such as visual and kinaesthetic. In which case, you could combine two approaches. Examples are

- Draw colourful pictures and walk around the room recalling them, or
- Pin your visual notes (poster-sized to A4) on a rough surfaced wall and trace the outline of your visual notes with your hands
- Sit in a different chair, at a different angle with a different view each time you look at particular notes.
- Sit in the same chair with the same view when you recall them.

If you check your *eye movement patterns* with this word list you will begin to have a clearer picture of the best learning and recall methods for yourself.

Techniques to match your senses
The three lists below bring together some examples of learning techniques which draw strongly upon your visual, aural (sound) and body (physical) learning senses. There is some cross-over between them and it is certainly a good idea to combine more than one sense to enhance the intensity of the image.

Visual techniques (seeing)
- Learning maps/mind maps/patterned notes (A4, A3 or poster-sized)
- Design a poster to capture the subject
- Use colour codes, eg on parts of formulae
- Use highlight pens for new information, different categories of information, eg tenses in French, different types of species in biology
- Check key word or flash cards
- Create a flow-chart
- Draw cartoons with facts attached
- Add facts and information to cut-out magazine pictures
- Use symbols and shapes like those on page 72 to give emphasis and variety.

Internal visualisations
You can also use visual techniques inside your head.
- Stop and take time to make a mental picture of what you are learning.

- Re-run a 'video' of what you have experienced through your imagination, picturing yourself in the situation and following with your video camera the sights, sounds and sensations as you move through the scene in your imagination – exactly as it happened.
- Bring up the poster you have drawn or the colourful A4 sheet of notes in your 'mind's eye' to refresh your memory.

Aural techniques (hearing)
- Make an audio-tape of a lecture, talk or TV programme.

- Explain a topic to someone else.
- Read aloud as if the topic is a drama.
- Write a jingle or a song or set what you want to remember to a suitable tune you know already.
- Talk to yourself – out loud and hear it in your head, a technique many writers use (see John Whale 1982).
- Make your own audio-tape of what you are learning, to play back to yourself in your room, on a personal stereo or in the car. It is useful for many things but excellent for languages, learning lines in plays and relaxation.

Body techniques (physical movement)
- Move around. Get up and talk to yourself as you walk.
- Write on Post-its and stick them on different objects.
- Demonstrate ideas by gesture and movement – with face, hands, arms and your whole body.
- Use quizzes and games to help you learn a topic.
- Role-play the issues with some of your peers.
- Place study materials in various places around your home.

Pay attention to detail
If you pay full attention to the detail of what you want to know or understand you will have a much better chance of recalling it.

One of the very best illustrations of how to use this insight to develop a skill is the step-by-step approach to drawing devised by Dorothy Edwards in her book *Drawing on the right side of the brain*. In it, she takes you through steps which involve you looking at an object from different perspectives such as drawing the object upside down (the object, not you) and touching the surface texture and shape of an object before drawing. She gives many illustrations of how individual people have transformed their drawing ability with such techniques (here rather briefly conveyed). I have also seen the results of people following her course from her writing: the results are impressive.

Combine sight and movement
There are two different approaches

- You can use this combination of senses to recall what you were learning and where. An example would be creating a patterned note with coloured pens on the economic ideas of Keynes whilst dangling your feet in water (in a pool, pond, stream or the sea).

- You can also create images of things you want to remember in your imagination by trying one or two of the following:

Picturing one or more objects
speeding along
flying
dancing
stuck <u>over</u>   or alongside another
     under
folded into each other
wrapped around another word, idea, picture
one inside another
crashing or smashing into another

Find a link with smell and taste
The technical term for smell is olfactory and the term for taste is gustatory and there is no doubt that they are powerful senses – perhaps the most powerful. We tend to overlook their importance and their potential to link with learning.

Some smells are particularly important. The perfume industry makes its fortune out of our interest and sensitivity to different fragrances. Such smells can 'turn our heads' or 'turn our stomachs' as can the smell of cooking 'make our mouth water'. You will notice that each of these phrases makes a link between smell and movement or other sensations.

Similarly some tastes are known to be particularly popular and sought after in many societies. Most people will have a reaction to bitter tastes. Imagine sucking a lemon or lime; what did you feel? Did your face move? Certainly sweet tastes spawn a huge world-wide industry of chocolate bars and sweets.

Some links between smell and sound are made accidentally such as when the smell of new-mown grass drifts to your nostrils at the same moment as you are listening to a poem in a classroom.

Devise you own list of smells and tastes to see if you can link some of them to particular pieces of information you want to remember. This could be something as simple as eating an orange or rubbing some favourite smell in the form of massage oil onto your hands as you read a passage in your book.

Moving and learning
One useful approach for connecting learning with the fullest range of your senses is to change the seat or position in which you are studying immediately after you have

• grasped some particular fact or understanding

- seen a way of applying an idea
- understood what you need to do next.

This would mean you moving around a room, occupying a slightly different position each time, ensuring that you do not return to the same place in a particular spell of study. In this way you both reinforce the learning and come to associate a particular piece of learning with a particular place.

Using several senses for peak performance

After winning a gold medal in the World Athletic Championships, Liz McColgan described what she did as she ran the 25 laps of 10,000 metres. 'I switch off. I visualise myself running alongside myself and running well. I listen to my body. I concentrate on the rhythm of my breathing and body. I take no notice of the laps. Toward the end I say to myself "I wish this was bloomin' over." '

Liz listens to her own body, cutting out much of the external world, illustrating the techniques described in *Listening on three levels*. She is also using a number of other approaches to enable peak performance. She is certainly using visualisation and rhythm, for example.

Use your eyes for visual recall

There are three parts to recalling an accurate picture of what you've just seen or read. The first part is to properly attend to it, checking you know how it looks. The second is to remain relaxed and calm, whilst recalling the picture, which is the third – and equally essential part. It is essential that in this stage you keep your eyes in a position above the horizon, ie you don't allow your eyes to drop down, for visual eye movements are upward eye movements. Most people picture a familiar scene eg the inside of their bedroom, by looking to the centre or to the left of the centre to recall the picture. You may find it helps to gaze into the distance, ignoring your surroundings or to close your eyes. Try it. If you try to recall the same scene with your eyes looking downward, is it as easy?

Exactly the same principle applies to trying to spell words accurately, for all good spellers are visual recallers. Test somebody who's a good speller and they'll either write it down on paper so they can see the word or they'll use an upward eye movement (often to the left of centre or to the centre distance) to read off the letters, or groups of letters of the word they've seen. You will find more details about eye movements on page 76.

Eye movements and recall

We now know that eye movements tell us how to access information. The faces below show you how you move your eyes to recall particular pictures, sounds and sensation.

Up or defocussed is for picturing (visualisation), eg picturing a page of notes; a place you know well; imagining a scene.

Down right is for feeling (sensation), eg you tend to look here when you are anxious or panicking; when you are recalling something you touched or tasted or smelt.

Anywhere else is for sound, eg talking to yourself, remembering what a tutor said, the words of a song, the script of a play.

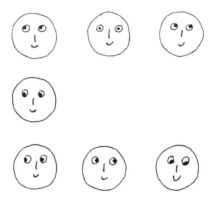

Here is another diagrammatic representation of the eye movement with some more specific indications of what is happening when you move your eyes in these directions.

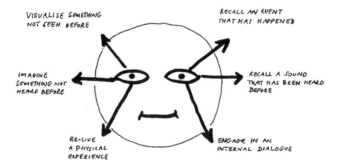

Use a friend to help you check eye movements
You can use a friend to help you check your own movements and can do the same for them.

● Notice that the way the faces are drawn is as if you look directly at the other person, so that eye movements which appear to be looking right on the page are actually the person looking left. Do, when you ask your friend questions, sit opposite them and notice very carefully where they move their eyes.

- Sometimes eye movements will not be clear to you, particularly if you become anxious. When you are anxious, your eyes will tend to move down.

You will remember best the information you can associate with positive images that are

- colourful
- moving/active
- 3-dimensional
- exaggerated

- funny
- distorted
- surreal
- absurd

- vivid
- sensual
- sexual
- erotic

and by associating the visual image with other senses whenever possible.

Imagine yourself as the object of your study
One research scientist has developed many of her new ideas by imagining herself as the tiny micro-organism into which she is researching. She sees herself setting out on a 'virtual-reality' journey and being faced by all the obstacles and dangers that the tiny particle will face. Partly as a result of this creativity she has become a world expert in this sphere of knowledge, contributing research papers and speaking at international conferences.

You can use this approach equally well to see yourself in the 'thick of the action' at some historical event or to imagine yourself travelling across some geographical landscape.

Shrink it
Take a little picture into the exam room
One tip for the exam room is to picture what you want to recall on a tiny piece of paper.

Imagine yourself taking it into the exam room with you on the back of your hand, for example, and being able to look at it in the exam room.

It is a technique to reassure you that you can take a picture with you into the exam room, a small, vivid one, and you can do it without cheating, without actually taking in a piece of paper.

MAKING WORD AND LETTER ASSOCIATIONS

Mnemonic devices
The word mnemonics comes from the Greek goddess of memory Mnemosyne. Mnemonics are devised for artificially aiding the memory. There are several of these, some of which are very familiar.

First letter mnemonics
Two examples – the colours of a rainbow/spectrum.
Richard Of York Gave Battle In Vain
Red Orange Yellow Green Blue Indigo Violet

Remember the sequence of
North East South West by linking them with Never Eat Shredded
Wheat

This can be combined with a visual image, moving clockwise around the circle.

The use of the first letter in a word to construct a more vivid, memorable sentence is used in several science subjects, eg Biology, as well as in subjects like History and Economics. *Words* can also be made from first letters.

Link mnemonics with humour
A mnemonic device with a slightly humorous or vulgar slant can be used to link one idea with another, as in

'Rene Descartes was a silly old fart
Who said I think therefore I am'

In this case linking a name of someone (Descartes) with an idea ('I think therefore I am'). You can use it equally well to link names with inventions or incidents and in physical or human science to link names with objects.

Rhymes
Familiar uses are for days of the month; 'Thirty days hath September, etc' and in the spelling rule 'i before e except after c'. You can invent your own rhymes or use those which exist already in a particular subject.

Spelling association
Where there is a confusion between the spelling of similar sounding words with different meanings, the correct spelling can be remembered by associating the spelling with that of an associated object, eg

stationary and stationery: stationery and envelopes.

When writing, I remember whether to use the word practice or practise by knowing that the two earlier letters in the alphabet go together, as do the two later ones ie c and n / s and v:

practice and noun, eg I went to the football practice
practise and verb, eg I practise deep breathing daily.

Number rhyme systems

This device is explained in Buzan (1984). A number is associated with an object with which it rhymes, eg four/door; five/hive. To remember a piece of information you link it with the number rhyme and create a picture which is as vivid, bizarre or humorous as possible involving the piece of information with the door or hive as the case may be.

Verbal association

Group words together, eg to remember port and starboard and their coloured lights on a boat:
Right – Starboard – Green are the three longer words,
Left – Port – Red are the three shorter words.

Pair words – Seek words that match/complement each other or are opposites to each other in order to aid the memory of both.

Link words and phrases with those already known to you.

Unlikely associations – Look for humorous, bizarre, exotic and colourful associations between facts, ideas and other information. Opposites can also be used as an aid to memory.

Make up a story – Form several words you want to remember into a story. The words appear in the story in the same sequence as you wish them to appear in answer to a question.

Using tape recordings to aid memory as you go to sleep

As you go to bed at night you can choose to use a tape recorder or personal stereo to play back some study ideas you have previously recorded. This is an opportunity to review the work you have been doing.

You can choose to add music to aid the absorption of what you have recorded by using the dubbing feature of a stereo system to record your voice over a previously recorded rhythm and/or soothing piece of music.

If you fall asleep whilst listening to some study material it may help your subconscious mind make links and associations in sleep. If sound in particular is an important way for you to access information, this technique may be worth trying: check your recall the following day and ask yourself, 'How much do I remember?'

Revising and remembering for problem solving (mathematically based) science and technology subjects

Repetition and mnemonics can both be used to learn formulae, tables, sequences etc. Other memorising ideas will suit particular topics or questions. Other particularly useful approaches are:

- To practise answering questions, both in *full* and in *outline*. Do this as often as possible. Worked examples and questions are a key approach in problem solving subjects.

- From an early stage, reduce the amount of time you allow yourself so that by the time you are close to the examinations you are allowing yourself no more time that you would have in the exam room.

- Practise diagrams and any other visual material without looking at the original book or notes. Upon completing them compare them with the original, repeating the process until you can draw an adequate representation of the original without errors.

- Use key word revision cards to practise recall of formulae, symbols, etc. and for keeping your diagram outlines.

- Let your imagination take off; picture yourself telling the story of the experiment, or how atoms interact by a fully financed major documentary. You can go anywhere and find any people, places, equipment or graphics you need to make a film that will vividly convey what scientist Dr Carol Turley calls the story-line.

- If you were making this documentary you would need a story-board, which is the sequence of the story-line, told in pictures. You would normally do these as small sketches, several to an A4 sheet, but you could also create a bigger image on poster-sized paper.

- Create a colourful poster. Group formulae together by colour codes – using colour to highlight *similarities* and *differences*.

Understanding and remembering maths

- Mathematics often makes sense if you picture the problem (upward eye movements) before you start to answer it. You could also make some guess as to the answer and as you work on it as to its conclusion. See how far off the correct answer you were initially.

- For learning formulae and other data, try creating the vivid and absurd images described on pp 77-78. You will find many concrete examples in Harry Lorayne (1992) (see **Further Reading and Help**).

- As you read maths questions, ask yourself 'What have I got to do with this?' The question-setter wants you to be able to unpick whatever has been set. As one Chief Examiner at GCSE put it 'Unpick the knitting to turn it into common-or-garden maths'. If you carefully read the question, circling key information and using coloured highlight pens, you will have made a good start by unpicking it.
- Use mnemonics like SOCATOA (say it aloud) for
  <u>S</u>ine – <u>O</u>pposite
  <u>C</u>osine – <u>A</u>djacent
  <u>T</u>angent – <u>O</u>pposite and <u>A</u>djacent
- Get used to writing out your workings in full even when you have used the calculator, by doing so after each step of the calculation. You can do this in pencil initially, because some mistakes almost inevitably occur. When you have the correct answer, you can write it out in full, in ink. From GCSE exams onwards, up to four out of every six marks can be given for those written workings and examiners say one of the most common mistakes is to miss them out.
- Maths is a 'building-block' subject in that you need to understand the bottom bricks in the wall before you can fit other ones onto them. It is best to start your revision from the points where you last clearly understood a particular 'brick' and how it fitted into the wall. Build up your confidence in a bit-by-bit 'brick-by-brick' way.

See, touch and learn

You can improve your understanding of a subject if there is an opportunity to see and touch a three-dimensional model. For example, a Podiatry student studying the bones of the foot for an examination to become a chiropodist, took home a model of the foot to practise on. By touching bones and seeing how one related to another, he was able to understand complex information more easily than in a drawing or two-dimensional diagram on a page.

Learning tables

In both maths and science you may find it helpful, even essential, to learn tables of information such as your *times tables*. Here are some approaches that may help you do it more effectively.

- Get an overall picture. Write out the tables on large sheets (even poster-sized) pieces of paper. Use different colours to indicate
  – those you know already (you usually do not have to start from scratch).
  – the ones you are going to learn next.

You can update this by changing the colours when you know you are able to recall it.

- Cooperate with someone else by saying the tables out loud. Sing or chant (in a rhythm) any parts you can.

- Record the tables onto a cassette and play them back to yourself, taking a section at a time.

- Cut up the tables into sections and spread them on the floor, tackling one at a time and forming a pile of those you now know.

- Walk around as you tackle or look at the information.

- Keep going over the information until you are sure you know it (repetition).

- Make up cards for parts of the tables and play test-yourself games – by yourself or with another person.

- Do not be bothered by the mistakes you make when learning them. If you make a mistake, find some simple 'soft and gentle' technique for picking it up eg a smile to yourself, a little whistle.

Want to know more?
You will find more about the techniques described in this chapter in the books and videos mentioned at the end of this book, in particular those by Dorothy Edwards, Tony Buzan, Joseph O'Connor and John Seymour, and Colin Rose, which cover such fields as drawing, mind-mapping, effective use of the brain, neuro-linguistic programming and accelerated learning.

5
Taking Exams

A WORD ABOUT EXAMS

Do exams have to be difficult?

In some ways you could argue that the first external-type examinations you take are the most difficult because they are unfamiliar and you have had little or no opportunity to develop any expertise in taking them. This would usually be GCSE exams such as French oral or Grades in music examinations. Many mature students returning to degree-level study in higher education find their first internally marked examinations cause them difficulties because they too are unfamiliar with exams after a long break from taking them.

You can minimise the unfamiliarity of these exams by simulating exam conditions and practising examination-type question and answer before you sit the exam: for many students, with experience and appropriate techniques, they can become easier. Overall, the difficulty of all examinations is exaggerated: exams are easier than is often believed.

Knowing your examinations

One way of checking that you know what each examination requires of you is to answer the following questions, where they apply to a subject.

(1) How many papers do you have to sit?
(2) What time is allowed for each paper?
(3) How many questions do you have to answer? How many questions are there to choose from?
(4) Do you have to answer questions from particular sections?
(5) Are there any compulsory questions?
(6) Are all questions worth equal marks? If not, which questions are worth more?
(7) What is the maximum time you could allow yourself for each question in order to divide your time equally?

Problem checklist

I have/may have problems with:	Tick if it applies to you	Brief tips	Where to find out more (pp.)
Knowing enough about what I have to do in the exams		Check you know the number of papers, questions and instructions to candidates. Are there any changes this year? Speak to your teachers/lecturers.	83-85
Getting started in the exam		Read instructions carefully. Read carefully through all the exam paper. Underline important words. Make brief answer plans.	93-98
Knowing which question to answer first		Most students answer their best question first. Examiners agree that this is a good idea.	100
Never having taken such an important exam before		You don't have to be brilliant to pass exams. Be positive. Know the standard expected of you beforehand.	88-92
Settling down in the exam room		Be methodical. Read instructions: have pens etc. ready. Read all questions. Learn some relaxation techniques in case they are needed.	93-94 128-137
Getting used to taking exams		Practise answering old exam questions in exam conditions with the same amount of time as in the exam.	87-89
Knowing what examiners are looking for		Examiners are looking to give marks, not to take them away. They are looking for answers that actually answer the question.	88-89
Knowing how much time to give to each question in the exam		Take away at least 30 mins. of a 3 hour exam for reading instructions, choosing questions, planning answers etc. Divide the rest of the time equally.	94-96
Fearing I will not be able to answer any questions when I read through the exam paper		This is often caused by reading through the paper too quickly. Read it again underlining all important words in each question. Learn to think more positively.	94-97 114-118
Making sure I reach each question properly		Underline words in questions. Try writing brief outline notes (linear or patterned) as a first answer to the question.	96-98
Wondering if I know enough to pass		Use the symbols described in **What should I revise?** Concentrate on what you are doing, not on worrying.	39-46 91-92
Wondering if I will be penalised for my spelling, handwriting or use of grammar		It is important to be legible with the minimum of grammar and spelling errors but examiners are often instructed not to penalise this unduly in exams.	78-79 104-105
Not being able to write fast enough; running out of time		Write in shorter sentences if you struggle to express yourself. Most people run out of time: timed questions will minimise the effect of doing so. Exercise your fingers – A Do-it-Yourself Guide to Muscular Relaxation.	104 128-137
Not answering all questions in full		If time is running out, answer two half-questions. This can gain more marks than one longer answer and a missed question.	94-96 104
Planning outline answers in the exam room		Practise this technique in revision as part of testing yourself. You do not have to write these outlines but they often help.	80 94-98

(8) How are marks proportioned between coursework (C), laboratory (L) or workshop (W), project work (P) and examinations (E)?

(9) Are marks linked between one year's examinations and another? (This occurs more frequently in some further and higher education exams).

(10) How long, at maximum, could you allow yourself for preparation in the exam, eg jotting down some outline answers?

If you don't know the answers to these questions, check with teachers and past papers, ensuring no changes have occurred since the last time candidates sat the examination.

Recording exam information

You can use this table to write down your answers to the ten questions on pp 83 and 85 for each examinable subject. Sub-divide subjects where there is more than one paper. Two examples are given as guidelines.

How to express your answer	As a number	In hours and minutes	No. Questions to answer No. Questions to choose from	Sections and numbers	(If applicable) Section and Q. No.	Note differences in marks, if any, where known	In minutes	In percentages	Yes/No Years/	Minutes
Subjects: two examples	Q1	Q2	Q3	Q4	Q5	Q6	Q7	Q8	Q9	Q10
Mathematics	1	2½ hr	10/14	Sect A-4 Sect B-3 Sect C-2	No	Equal	12-15 mins	E 100%	No	20-30 mins
Geography	1	3 hrs.	5/9	Sect A-1 Sect B-2 Sect C-2	Q1 Sect A	Q1 = 40% Others = 15% ea.	Q1- 50-60 mins Others 20-25 mins	P = 20% E = 80%	Yr 1 = 30% Yr 2 = 70%	30-40 mins
Your Exam Subjects										

MAKING CONTINGENCY PLANS

It will benefit you to make plans before the exams begin, particularly if you anticipate difficulties.

Health

Health issues are one obvious example where you can sometimes anticipate difficulties.

Suffering from hay fever?
If you are a hay fever sufferer you are particularly at the mercy of the pollen count in the summer examination months of May and June.

You are likely to be given medical guidance by your GP which would include some combination of tablets, nasal spray and eye drops. There may still be some problem of drowsiness associated with taking some of these products; it is worth checking this with your doctor.

Even with the best preparation you may still find yourself on a hot day with a high pollen count when the windows are open in the examination room and someone starts cutting the lawn outside. If some such event occurs or you do suffer from drowsiness because of your medication, make sure you inform the invigilator at the end of the examination and the appropriate examination board. They can take such problems into account once your paper is marked.

Period pains
Period pains would be another example where medical help beforehand, eg pain killers, may reduce problems.

It may be appropriate as well to inform your examination centre ie normally your school or college, if your symptoms are apt to be severe. They are able to inform the Examining Boards of any information you pass on. Your papers will be marked in the usual way and then any information from the Centre will be considered. Exactly the same principle applies to illness that occurs in the examination room.

Tell someone if you're not well. There may be a system in your school, college or university where you can fill in a form to inform key people.

Equipping yourself

Get ready any spare pens and any other equipment you need the day before. Put them in the bag you will take with you to the exam next day. There are usually clear guidelines as to what equipment you can take with you into exams, so check this beforehand.

For maths-type examinations from GCSE onward, you will need equipment such as a pencil, ruler, eraser, protractor, and calculator.

Don't borrow another unfamiliar and more complicated calculator at the last moment. You may find you are wasting valuable time in trying to use it properly. Also with calculators, take a spare battery with you in case it chooses the time of the exam to run out of energy!

Sometimes formulae are printed on the examination paper at GCSE level. Check with your school or college to see if this is the case and which ones you are given.

Arriving late

You would normally be allowed, by most examination regulations, to enter any room up to half-an-hour late, if you find yourself delayed. *If you do arrive late*, do not allow yourself to be panicked. Stick to a revised and foreshortened time budget with the aim of attempting *all* the questions you have been asked to complete.

Knowing the place and time

Finding out exactly *where the exam is held*, how long it takes to reach the place, and exactly what time the examination begins and ends will enable you to plan in advance. For example, you will be able to note actual times for reading the paper, answering the first question, beginning the second and subsequent questions.

Coping with anxiety

Learning and practising the *relaxation, positive thinking and panic coping* techniques in the **Coping with Anxiety** chapter will also prepare you for all eventualities in the examination room.

GETTING USED TO EXAMS

Although some people appear to take examinations in their stride, for the rest of us the feelings associated with examinations make it very difficult to get used to them. However, if we can familiarise ourselves with what is expected of us beforehand, it may well help to lessen their impact upon us and enable us to cope better in the examination room.

Know what the examination examines

Use the guidelines in **Know your examination** and **Recording exam information** to get a clear picture of the structure of the examination.

Add to this conversations with teachers/lecturers for their guidelines; looking at the syllabus (when it is available); surveying all your notes and other work from the course; reviewing past exam papers and making use of the ideas in **Devise questions around a topic** (p 46).

Practise answering questions in examination conditions

Simulate examination conditions by answering a question *in silence without* the aid of *books or other materials; at a desk* and within strictly applied *examination time limit.* You can do this for:

- individual questions
- a whole paper (2, 2½ or 3 hours)
- planning outline answers (linear, spider or patterned notes).

This will provide practice at thinking clearly and quickly in examination conditions. You may wish to try these approaches gradually, eg giving yourself less time each time to answer the question; working for a longer silent period each time. You could add to this:

- using a friend or parent as an invigilator, so you can get used to someone walking past you or standing behind you
- sitting in the room where you will sit the exam to get the feel of it.

Learn from mock exams or tests

Once you have completed your mock exams, engage in a full post-mortem of them by yourself or with the help of another. Whether they went well or badly, use the **Problem Checklists** to analyse what happened. Check your revision, exam techniques and your anxiety levels. *Write down* the changes you will make and start to put them into operation immediately.

Know the standard expected of you

You don't have to be brilliant to pass examinations or to do very well in them. Here are some guidelines to help you:

Standards expected
- Comments as well as marks on your work during the course.
- Any examples of model answers by lecturers, teachers or Examination Boards. These may also come from good answers to questions by other students known to you.

Standards that students have used
- The average student who completes an average amount of course work, expends an average amount of effort and develops an average understanding should pass the exam.
- By revising half the syllabus, the candidate will be able to answer around half the questions in the exam and with half marks gained on each will pass.

Neither of these two guidelines are exactly accurate. They could, in fact, by misleading. If the 'average' students in your group have not yet achieved a pass standard in their work, the first guideline is unlikely to be true. It is possible to revise half the syllabus but omit to revise some of the most important, and frequently occurring, topics in which case the second guideline is unlikely to be true. There are, too, other exceptions, eg certain medical or Taxation professional examinations where a high degree of technical knowledge and understanding is demanded.

However, the *spirit* of these two statements is very useful. It is that *the vast majority of examinations are not as difficult as students believe them to be.*

And an examiner comments

One examiner's point confirms the emphasis of **The importance of asking questions** (p 8).

'A worrying number of candidates totally misread the question and thus misdirected the answer.

'The most persistent weakness was a failure to answer the question actually asked: too many candidates preferred to answer the question they would have liked to have been asked or even just put down everything they knew.'

Remember the good news

Examiners are not looking for weaknesses or inadequacies, they are looking to give marks – they want candidates to pass. The red pen is poised to tick not to cross or slash through what you've written but to find what is competent, clear, correct, relevant and creditable in what you've written.

DISPEL IRRATIONAL BELIEFS ABOUT EXAMS

Here are six common beliefs that are held about exams and their outcome, each of which have some elements of false assumption or irrationality in them.

My future will be ruined if I fail/fail to get the grades I want

Examinations are an important way in which professional groups in our society select for their membership. Success in them does open doors to particular jobs and careers. Lack of success will mean certain jobs and careers are not immediately open to you, at least at the level of entry you originally intended. Some may be closed altogether.

However, happiness, wealth, peace of mind, rich experience of life,

Know what examiners want – and don't want

Examiners DO want	Examiners DO NOT want
To give marks. Examiners are often teachers and lecturers sympathetic to students. In many internal exams they will be your own lecturers and teachers, with good reason to seek to award you marks.	To take marks away. (Examiners are not poised with pens ready to penalise your mistakes).
You to pass.	You to fail.
You to answer the question that has been set.	Waffle and bluffing which may irritate them: to be told all the candidate knows about a topic, whether it answers the question or not.
You to present the best of what you have done.	To know what you haven't done.
You to demonstrate what you understand and its relevance to the question.	Indiscriminately writing all you know stuffing facts and figures you have memorised into an answer.
Scripts to be legible. They have a large number to read in a short time with the same fee for each script.	Illegibility. See **Legibility.**
All the required number of questions to be attempted.	Extra questions to be attempted. Not only do they not gain more marks, but the reverse is usually true as answers tend to be shorter. Fewer than the required number of questions to be attempted. They are disappointed for the candidate.
Short, simple sentences and a direct style of writing.	Over-elaborateness, over-wordiness.
Opinions to be backed by relevant argument.	Unsubstantiated opinion, ie 'I think' or 'I believe' without adequate explanation or argument for the belief. In Social Science, the use of 'I. . .' in this manner is frequently frowned upon and opinions are expressed impersonally.
All parts of a question to be answered.	You to neglect the second part of a question, which is frequently worth the same marks as the first part. (A common fault of candidates).
Appropriate examples and illustrations.	A catalogue of examples before a point is properly explained.
Standard English.	The use of slang or spoken expressions, particularly at the beginning of sentences eg 'Yes, you can please some of the people. . . ', 'Well . . .', 'As I was saying. . . '.
You to answer the question immediately you start to write.	You to copy out the question, unless you are specifically asked to do so. Long background introductions to the topic.
Humour – intentional or unintentional!	To be bored by a candidate who has evidently put in little effort.
A structure to your answer, ie a beginning, middle and end with a number of separate paragraphs in written answers.	A written answer without paragraphs, lacking structure or a clear story-line.

Other guidelines are provided in **Writing essay-type answers** meaningful status in the eyes of others, a worthwhile career, a useful job and an inner sense of purpose and self belief as a human being, do not depend upon examination results. The world is teeming with people who have found that to be the case whether they passed examinations or not.

I am not lucky with exams
Some people do appear luckier than others at games of chance, with acquiring money, in making relationships or in achievements. There is certainly an aspect of chance involved in which questions appear on the examination paper compared to those you have chosen to revise.

However, examination technique can be learned very effectively by anybody and the element of luck reduced to a minimum. Practising what you have to do in the exam room is the key, as Arnold Palmer, one of the most successful golfers of all time, is quoted as saying: 'The more I practise, the luckier I seem to get.'

I'm just no good at exams. Some people are; I'm not
There are two elements in this view. One is that our past performance will determine any future attempts. The other is in comparing yourself to others you find your performance inadequate. The answer to the first element is that the past frequently *is* escapable. By buying this book and reading this page, you have set out to become 'good at exams'. Other people are largely irrelevant. They do not depend for their success upon your lack of success or vice versa.

Exams get more difficult as you work your way up
Difficulty is a relative word. What is difficult at one age is not at another; what is difficult when you are inexperienced in an activity is not when you are experienced; what is difficult to one person is not to another; what is difficult on one day is not on another.

Certainly, examinations demand more specialist knowledge, understanding and expertise, as you move through their different levels. They may become more technical, involve more abstract ideas and concepts, involve you in greater specialisation and more specialist jargon. This does not mean they become more difficult.

I haven't covered the syllabus so I won't pass
It isn't irrational to fear that you haven't revised or understood enough of the subject you have studied to pass a course. It may be true that if you have studied and revised little of the course you have left yourself at risk of failing to accumulate sufficient marks to pass it. It may be that you will need some luck in the choice of questions that appear in the

exam paper.

However, it is irrational to believe that if you haven't covered the syllabus you are inevitably going to fail the course. Few courses, teachers or students 'cover the syllabus' in the sense of paying full and equal attention to all parts of it. Examiners do not expect you to have done so. They accept that there are bound to be areas where you are underprepared, unclear or uninformed. They want to see you demonstrate what you do understand and what you have prepared.

Even when you are struggling to find enough questions to answer, you will find that many have some kind of link or association with your course content. You will normally find some links which you can build up into an answer.

The exams will expose me as a phoney or stupid

You may experience the common fear in many students that the exams will expose them as inadequate, lacking in even basic know-how or understanding. There is a further underlying fear – that the exams will expose your lack of ability to be tackling that level of study, whether it be GCSE or post-graduate qualifications. The fear can be further intensified by fantasies of the judgement by examiners, tutors, family and friends. Examiners can be seen as poised with red pens to expose your ignorance and misunderstanding. You may feel that family and friends see you as stupid or that tutors will reject you as they feel let down or fooled.

As I have argued in **Why I wrote this book**, the focus on ability is largely irrelevant. The vast majority of people who set off on a course of study are quite *capable* of successfully completing it. It is practical life circumstances, false beliefs and negative attitudes which, coupled with poor study techniques, may cause the problems – not lack of ability.

USING THE LAST FEW HOURS

On the night before the examination

- Review your key word cards with the emphasis on practising recall. Attempting to cram in *new* material, although tempting, will tend to use up energy and be self-defeating.

- Check you have all the equipment – pens, pencils, instruments, etc. you need and are allowed to take into the exam room. Several different shaped pens may ease the pressure points on your fingers and thumbs.

- Check the timetable as to the right time and place of the exam. Make sure you have any candidate's number or any other administrative items you need.

- Check your personal timetable for the next morning, checking the times you need to get up, gather your materials, leave the house, etc.

- Use any of the ideas you have developed from the **Coping with Anxiety** chapter to aid your relaxation and to sleep.

On the day of the examination

- Try as far as possible to stick to your normal routine.

- If you do normally eat breakfast, take it as normal for you will be using up a considerable amount of energy. If you don't eat breakfast normally, consider eating something light. If this does not seem possible, you could consider taking some glucose tablets, barley sugar or mints with you for the examination room: for most external examinations unobtrusive sweet sucking would be permitted.

- Don't drink too much in the morning. Part of the normal reaction to exams is a state of appropriate nervous tension and arousal you may feel. This may well cause more visits to the lavatory than usual, which is a perfectly normal – and appropriate – reaction. You don't, however, want the need to continue in the exam room, if it can be avoided!

- Check your personal timetable made the night before to ensure all is going to time, occupying spare time you have constructively by doing something positive or relaxing.

- Check you have all your equipment before you leave home.

- You can take brief looks at your revision card summaries, re-checking your recall.

- Use the deep breathing and other relaxation techniques when you feel the need for them. You may also find the ideas in **On the way to the Exam** and **The morning before an afternoon exam** helpful (see p 122).

STARTING YOUR EXAM

Getting settled

Settle and compose yourself. Set out any pens, pencils, rulers, rubbers, and other permitted equipment. Check your watch with the clock in the room, which should be visible to you. If it is not visible to you, place your watch where you can easily see it. This is the moment to practise all the ideas for positive alert performance described in the **Coping with Anxiety** chapter, eg **Visualising the examination.**

Read right through the paper

Read right through the exam paper. *Allow yourself at least five minutes for this. In particular, re-check that the instructions are as you expected as in* **Know your examinations, Recording exam information**. *Note* the length of the exam and write down the finishing time: any compulsory questions; the number of questions to be answered in total and from which sections of the paper they are to be selected.

If you tend to be anxious about finding your hoped-for question appearing in the examination paper, read through the paper *not expecting* the questions you want to appear. *Expect* it to be difficult to find enough questions to answer. Adopting this approach you will probably find your hopes raised rather than dashed and it will help you look at each question much more carefully. This is not designed to be the opposite of a positive approach, simply a steadying, realistic approach.

Pay particular attention to what the question is asking. It is very easy to jump to incorrect conclusions about the meaning of a question. A common explanation for this is anxiety to find certain topics or questions causes *a word or phrase* to be selected from a question and assumed to be the topic or particular question. We want to find certain questions so we *do* them, whether or not they are really worded as we wish them to be! In the same way, other questions, which may well be more appropriate questions to choose, are dismissed because a key word or phrase does not appear when it is said quickly for the first time.

One way to prevent this happening is to develop the technique of **Underlining key words in questions** (pp 96-97).

One outcome of underlining can be to discover that simply worded questions are not always the easiest to attempt. Questions which require careful reading can be easier for you to answer once you have clearly understood them.

Plan your time

You can plan the outline of the time you will allocate in an exam, before the day of the examination. If you **Know your examinations** and know the start and finishing times you can make a rough plan of your time allocation. During the examination itself, write down the planned finishing time for each question. Divide the time according to marks allocated per question and marks allocated per part of a question. (Increasingly, Examination Boards are including this information).

- Stick to your time budget. As explained in **If you are running out of time**, two half-answered questions will usually obtain more marks than one completed question and one unanswered question.

Techniques in the exam room

The outline is expanded and adapted from one used by Rowntree (1976), in his useful book *Learn how to study.*

Settle and compose yourself
Lay out your equipment, at least two pens, ruler, pencil and other permitted equipment.

Read right through the paper (5 minutes)
Check instructions very carefully. How many questions – from each section?
Underline key words in questions.
Choose your best questions, using a symbol system.
Analyse the question very carefully, checking whether it is a 'What' or 'How' type question or a 'Why' type.

Plan your time
Divide according to marks per question.
Write down finishing time for each question.
If possible, plan in 10 minutes checking time at end.

Plan your answers
Brief notes on main ideas and important details.
Linear, spider or pattern note outline.
Outline all answers at beginning (if doubtful of remembering); or one at a time or a few answers together.
Leave space after each question.
Ignore other candidates writing speed and spare paper collecting – it is irrelevant to your performance.

Priorities
Answer your best question first.
Stick to the time allowed for each question: marks for two half-questions are work more than one.
Stick to what the questions are asking.

Write
Simply, in short sentences, checking spellings.
Legibly.
Avoiding long 'background' introductions.

At the end of the exam:
If there is time left, check your answers.
Minimise your conversations.

• Use any time remaining at the end of the exam to check your answers for 10 minutes. Many students never have this checking time at the end and it is by no means essential that you plan it in.

Plan your answers

You can use brief notes to outline an answer to the question. You may decide that you would prefer to get straight on with your answer. As long as you have a clear idea of what you wish to write in your answers there is no problem with this approach. You should do what suits you best.

• You can find examples of outline notes in **Using underlined words to form an outline answer** and in **Spider diagrams** and **Pattern notes** (see p. 97).

• If you are using this type of outlining plan, it can be a useful approach to outline all your answers in one working spell at the beginning of the exam. Alternatively, you can plan one answer at a time or two or three together before commencing to write out your full answers. The advantage of planning all your answers at the beginning is that it enables you to record a considerable amount of information whilst it is fresh in your mind; it removes the anxiety that you will forget it by the time you come to answer a later question. It also gives you notes to fall back on if you run out of time. In an emergency, you could refer the examiner to them, if they are readable and comprehensible. You can also add to these notes during the course of the exam when you think of other points you have remembered: answering one question often throws up associations with another topic or question.

• Leaving spaces after each answer will enable you to add to it, if you recall more information.

• Do not allow yourself to get stuck on a stubborn problem. Return to it later. A change of question can often enable you to gain a fresh perspective on the previous question.

Underlining key words in questions

Answering an exam question correctly depends upon understanding it clearly in the first place. A useful technique is to underline, after careful consideration, the most important words, phrases or data in the question. See page 97 for an example.

Although you often end up underlining most of the words in question, it is where the lines are drawn and where the spaces between lines occur which draws your attention to the exact meaning of the question.

If the words which tell you the type of question are underlined twice (or in a different colour), it will ensure you take the right approach with your answer.

In conclusion, this technique has several advantages:

- It ensures you read the question properly and note exactly what it is asking. It is very easy, in your anxiety to find a question you can answer and to get started, to misread a question. This can cause you to ignore a question which it would be quite possible for you to answer and to choose to answer a question which turns out to be different from your original perception of it.

- It draws your attention to the approach that examiners want you to take, ie the type of question it is.

- It provides you with the key words to start a brief outline answer plan.

An example
Q.1 <u>Give an account</u> of the <u>digestion</u>, <u>absorption</u> and <u>use</u> of <u>carbohydrates.</u>

- In order to test whether you have underlined the correct words to enable you to fully and exactly understand the question say the words you have underlined quietly aloud to yourself.
- Practise this underlining technique with questions from past papers or questions you are currently answering.

Using underlined words to form an outline answer
You can use the underlined words to form an outline answer, either in linear or pattern/spider form.

Using a patterned or spider outline

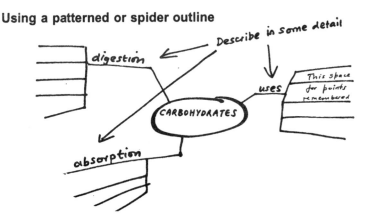

Using a linear plan

You would list the key points under headings of *digestion, absorption* and *uses*.

UNDERSTANDING THE TYPES OF QUESTION

Questions in examinations vary in the approach they ask you to take. In every question there are certain key words (a number of these are verbs) which tell you the type of question it is and exactly which approach the examiner wishes you to take.

Two common groupings are descriptive and analytical questions. Below are listed fifteen descriptive and nineteen analytical words and phrases which occur commonly. Each is then defined.

Descriptive questions

Define – set down the precise meaning of a word or phrase. Show that the distinctions implied in the definition are necessary.

Describe – give a detailed or graphic account of.

Distinguish between – note the difference between.

Give an account of – describe in some detail.

How . . . – in what way, by what means or method, to what extent.

Illustrate – use a figure or diagrams to explain or clarify, *or* make it clear by the use of concrete examples.

Outline – describe without detail, summarise.

Relate – narrate (the more usual meaning in examinations): to show how things are connected and to what extent they are alike or affect each other.

State – present in brief, clear form.

Show how – make clear by what means.

Summarise – give a concise account of the chief points or substance of a matter, omitting details and examples.

Trace – follow the development or history of a topic from some point of origin.

What . . . – of which kind, which?

When . . . – at what time, on which day or year, etc.?

Where . . . – at/to what place, in what particular?

Analytical questions

Account for – explain.

Analyse – make a detailed description and criticism of.

Argue the case for – back your opinion by reasoning in favour of it.

Assess – determine the amount of value of.

Calculate – reckon or compute by mathematics.

Comment upon – offer an opinion (avoiding the use of 'I. . .').

Compare – look for similarities and differences between.

Consider – express your thoughts and observations about.

Contrast – set in opposition in order to bring out differences.

Criticise – give your judgment about the merit of theories or opinions or about the truth of facts, and back by a discussion of the evidence.

Discuss – investigate or examine by argument, giving reasons pro and con.

Evaluate – make an appraisal of the worth of something, in the light of its truth or utility.

Examine – inquire into, attempt to discover, investigate.

Explore – approach in a questioning manner.

Explain – make plain, interpret, account for, illustrate the meaning of.

Interpret – expound the meaning of; make clear and explicit; usually giving your own judgment also.

Justify – show adequate grounds for decisions or conclusions.

Review – to make a survey of, examining the subject critically.

Why . . . – for what reason(s).

Other types of question

Some questions combine both types of question as the examiner looks for a combination of facts and analysis, as in 'Describe and explain'.

Quotations usually indicate some kind of analysis is required.

'*Brief*' or '*List*' mean what they say. A paragraph for the first and a straightforward descriptive list, such as that above.

'*Compare and Contrast*' type questions require you to point out the similarities and differences between two items, events or ideas. A good answer would focus on one aspect at a time and find the differences and similarities.

An example – Q. Compare and Contrast cars and motorbikes.

The same applies for 'For and Against' type questions, where, although you can argue all the points 'for' and then all the points, 'against' separately the answers which effectively argue for and against aspect-by-aspect can be the most successful.

In social science subjects such as History, Sociology and Economics, it is important to distinguish whether the examiner is asking you about the causes or reasons for or whether you are being asked about the results of events or actions.

- 'Factors', 'Account for', 'What problems faced?' – suggest you should write about reasons and causes.
- 'Achievements', 'Effects', 'Impact', 'How successful', 'The importance of' – suggest you should write about the results or consequences of an event, an idea or action.

Choosing the questions you will answer

Use some simple symbol systems to indicate your reaction to each question, once you have carefully read it and decided exactly what it is asking.

Guidelines that can be used are:

- Use a simple star system (up to 3 or 5 stars ***) next to each question: Choose the questions with the highest star rating.
- Use the EASY/DIFFICULT and KNOW/UNDERSTAND symbols from **Deciding what to revise?** choosing those questions on the positive end of scale.
- Give the questions scores out of 10 to indicate your confidence in answering them.
- Number the questions in the order you will answer them, choosing your best question first; then second best, third best and so on.

Writing essay-type answers

You cannot exactly reproduce in the exam room an essay you wrote on the same question as part of your coursework. The time constraints in an exam are different and a more direct precise style is more appropriate for most examinations.

Here are some of the principal guidelines.

- Try to lay out your answer so that it looks attractive, particularly where your comprehension of the English language is being tested.
- Do not waste time copying out the question (unless asked).
- Write in continuous prose, not notes.
- Decide whether it is a descriptive or analytical essay you are being asked to write. Use **Underlining key words** and **Types of questions** to help you decide.
- Keep your essay plan close by so that you can refer to it with ease.
- Avoid repetition, vagueness, generalisations and waffle.
- Use short paragraphs as well as simple, shorter sentences.

Exam essays have a beginning, a middle and an end. The beginning *Introduction* will have several of these features:

- a summary of what you are about to argue or describe
- an indication of your attitude to the question asked
- the key words from the question incorporated into the above, to indicate that you have read and understood the question
- a back-up reason for any first statements made, this can be expanded upon or added to in the middle
- definitions of any terms that clearly need to be defined in order for you to proceed with your answer.
- it will be one or two paragraphs long
- it will indicate that more needs to be described, explained or argued to clarify what has been said so far
- state how you interpret the title ie what do you understand by it?
- briefly outline the ideas, factors or arguments you are going to consider and why.

But don't
- give your answers to the questions in the title in the introduction. These fit in the conclusion.
- simply write out the question again in your introduction but refer to the key phrase.
- give simple dictionary definitions of terms. Use more authoritative definitions.

Writing a model essay
Introductions to essays are often of a very poor standard. Some candidates obviously get stuck in trying to express themselves. You can feel they are wondering what to write. Others simply re-state the title and say something like 'I will now go on to answer the question': a poor start. Yet others start a long, long background account of a situation, event, period, etc before beginning to make any relevant points in answer to the question. So I would suggest if you find introductions to essays difficult you try some of these alternatives:

- Practise them before the exam, using the principles outlined.
- Write a very short, one or two sentence, introduction before moving on to the essential core of the essay – the middle part.
- Don't waste time thinking of 'special' things to say in an introduction. Get on with answering the question in a straightforward manner, using your plan.

The middle
The middle will normally contain your key facts. They will be expressed precisely and specifically and in as much detail as the question appears

to demand. Try to avoid generalisations or covering up phrases which attempt to conceal that you can't remember a piece of information.

Assemble your major facts in a clear manner and show how they are relevant to the answer. Where the essay involves you arguing a case, citing reasons, explaining causes, analysing consequences and other forms of analysis, let the facts support your arguments.

The end – your conclusion

Concluding paragraphs are often as inadequate as introductions! As with introductions it is best not to think of them as being special concluding paragraphs.

Ideally, you will reach a coherent logical conclusion at the end of your essay. It does not have to side with any particular issue that the question focuses on. You can argue that the evidence is conflicting, the fors and againsts evenly balanced or that evidence is insufficient. Practise this type of conclusion in your preparation for the examination.

In your conclusion

- read the title again before you write it to ensure your conclusion has the emphasis the title required
- summarise the main points
- answer the question in the title or comment upon what the title required.

If you find concluding paragraphs difficult, don't over-concern yourself with them. Simply answer the question to the best of your ability and when you have do so – stop.

Finally, in conclusion, try not to start your final paragraphs with 'Finally. . .' or 'In conclusion . . .' It is boring, repetitive and tends to cause examiners to yawn!

It is important to remember that the bulk of marks in the vast majority of essay-type questions are awarded to the quality of the information and argument that forms the middle of most answers.

Answering multiple-choice questions and objective tests

The use of multiple-choice examinations is on the increase, although essay-type examinations remain the most common.

Multiple-choice questions, as their name implies, give you a choice of answers to a specific question. By marking a box, in the way you are instructed, you indicate which answer best fits the question. In this way, the multiple-choice exam aims to reward a good grasp of the whole syllabus without placing an undue emphasis upon the candidate's ability to write descriptive answers.

The main points to bear in mind in answering this type of question are:

- Read the instructions particularly carefully, the time you are allowed and how to complete the answers. As many of these tests and exams are marked by computer it is important that you actually complete your answers in exactly the form required.

- Work straight through the paper, noting the more difficult questions which you can return to later. Once you are sure you have the right answer, don't spend time re-considering.

- Underline key words in the questions to ensure you have read them properly. Particularly be on the lookout for *not* and double negatives in objective tests.

- Pick the alternative that appears to be nearest the truth. Multiple-choice tests are not purely tests of factual recall. They also test your comprehension and interpretation of information. One statement is going to be closest to the truth. By eliminating the answers you know to be wrong you will limit your choice and improve your chance of answering correctly.

- Don't guess randomly, but make informed guesses when you do not know. However, you should check the marking system, whenever possible, to see if incorrect answers are penalised. If penalties apply, as they do in a number of objective tests, but less often in multiple-choice papers, then be wary of guessing. Leave the difficult questions until later and return to them after completing the section. Reflecting on the question may give you some insight into the answer.

- Multiple-choice papers are not speed tests as such, but do require you to work at a business-like speed. Don't spend a long time puzzling over one or two questions. Continue on through the paper as questions you find easier may well occur throughout the paper. With other objective tests, timed sections do require that you work quickly. Keep your watch in view to time yourself carefully.

Preparing for an oral exam

The secret of good preparation for an oral examination in a foreign language such as French or in some fields of medicine is to be very thoroughly prepared.

You can do this by

- practising the key phrases you will use to begin sentences
- practising the key information, terms and phrases you will use
- testing yourself with another person asking you questions in the role of 'the examiner'
- rehearsing as many times as you can and simulating the examination situation
- learning upward eye movements to minimise panic (see p 76)
- using your senses to the full when learning the materials (see p 69)
- starting off each of your rehearsals and preparation sessions by being in a composed state.

OVERCOMING COMMON EXAM PROBLEMS

If you are running out of time

Divide whatever time that remains between questions. Examiners share a wide measure of agreement that it is easier to gain five marks in the last questions than an extra five in the question you were last working on. For this reason, two half answered questions usually gain more marks than one more completely answered question with which you have persevered.

With 10 minutes left and one answer to complete, you may revert to an emergency technique. Use brief notes to answer a descriptive (word-based) question. Minimise the amount of calculation shown in mathematically-based problem solving subjects. (NB This latter guideline may not apply equally to students in higher education, where showing all understanding of the means of calculation may be an important source of marks.)

Provided these brief outlines are readable and comprehensible to the examiner, they can gain marks. In most examinations, Examining Boards lay down criteria for marking brief notes, on a reduced scale of marks.

Alternatively, if you have written readable notes of skeleton outlines at the beginning of the examination, you can refer the examiner to them as your time elapses. If you do this, cross out the work you do not wish the examiner to read (a good principle at the end of an examination).

Legibility

It is a help to examiners if your handwriting is clear and readable. They will not deliberately penalise illegible handwriting, but examiners are human beings and they are going to be irritated if, because of difficulty in reading your handwriting, it takes them two or three times as long to read your script as it does to read another candidate's script of similar length, content and quality.

As with spelling and grammar, most Examining Bodies give guidelines to examiners as to how they should treat such scripts and, where penalties are imposed, they will tend to be only a small proportion of the total marks awarded in many examinations, eg 5-10%.

However, even if your handwriting is not particularly legible, you could considerably improve its legibility by:

– spacing it out more
– making sure you have no two letters that look exactly alike
– avoiding loops which overlap above and below the line.

Writing style
Writing style is not a key factor in most examinations, unless it is a subject where you are examining literature or grammatical style, eg English Literature and Language.

You may wish to impress the examiner with the fluency of your writing and will probably do so, if you succeed. However, it is not desirable to sacrifice facts and arguments for style. Whenever you find yourself with difficulties in expressing yourself, write in short, direct, simple sentences. This is a useful guideline for most examination answers.

COPING WITH THE AFTERMATH

The problem with analysing what you write with friends or others is that, in my experience, nearly everybody is equally convinced they have missed out key facts, answered questions in the wrong way, miscalculated etc. As a result such port-mortem discussions invariably reduce confidence and serve little purpose. In addition, your memory of what you wrote and its standard is likely to be imperfect, even if your recall is good. The difference between what you remember you wrote and exactly what you wrote can make a significant difference to the marks you obtain.

In some circumstances it can be useful to discuss certain issues. For example, where a subject is examined by two separate papers, the topics and types of question which appear in the first can give you guidelines to the topics and questions which may appear in the second paper.

And if the results are not what you hoped . . .
If you don't pass the examination on this occasion, it does not mean you're stupid or that you've wasted people's time even if some people believe that to be true. They are entitled to their misperceptions.

If you don't pass the examination with the performance you were hoping for or even expecting then over time there is an opportunity to learn from the experience by

- looking at your learning techniques
- thinking again about your choice of course or subject
- checking over how well you prepared yourself
- examining your exam technique

and

- reviewing how you manage yourself and your lifestyle.

There is nearly always something positive you can gain from the experience. In one sense there is no such thing as success or failure, only *feedback* (information for you to act upon in the future). I have met hundreds of people who have transformed their lives after 'failure' or disappointment; the comments in **Dispel irrational beliefs about exams** are very relevant (pp 89-90).

6
Coping with Anxiety

UNDERSTANDING WORRY, ANXIETY AND STRESS

It is a natural human reaction to worry at times during your studies. It is also natural to express an emotional reaction to the ups and downs of tackling tasks; angry or frustrated at one time, exhilarated at another.

The ideas in this book are intended to help you avoid becoming locked into a state of anxiety, where your interaction with exams, tests and course deadlines (the potential 'stressors') results in an unhelpful stress reaction in you. This is the type of anxiety state which feels disabling.

If you have found yourself feeling overwhelmed by this form of anxiety, then there are hundreds of ideas here to help you unpick it and move you into an emotional state in which you are able to think, feel and tackle study tasks with a feeling of your own power and well-being.

Achieving optimum arousal

The trick is to find the right level of arousal. Too little or too much arousal can bring problems. What you need is to be actively involved in your own learning to ensure you are engaged enough with what you are doing to move things from your short-term to long-term memory. In doing this you can actually enjoy what you are doing; it does not have to hurt for real learning to be taking place. It can enable you to be more alert, attentive and to concentrate more fully. It can sharpen your exam performance; make you feel more full of energy; cause you to work at the most effective speed and be more attentive to detail.

It is possible to mistake this state of arousal for anxiety. It is also possible for anxiety to become disabling, ie to stop you working effectively or at all. Equipped with the practice of these ideas, you will be able to cope with your anxiety, no matter how severe or overwhelming it feels using brain arousal to bring you to peak performance.

Problem checklist

I have/may have problems with	Tick if it applies to you	Brief tips	Where to find out more (pp)
How anxious to be before an exam		Some tension and nervous energy can be useful to trigger you to action.	107
How to cope with panic before or during the exam		Learn *An emergency quick relaxation technique, Create a scene in your imagination* and *Breathing slowly and deeply*	128-129 140
Being unable to concentrate		See *Improving concentration*. Practise focusing your attention during revision, cutting out distracting sounds	24-25 143
Getting to sleep at night		Exercise, warm baths, relaxation exercises and a good sleeping posture can all be useful.	123-128
How to relax in the exam room		Learn techniques of muscle tensing and relaxing as well as how to breathe to relax	128-137
Whether to take some time off for relaxing and entertainment		Definitely. Incorporating time off into your revision programme is a part of your revision time not a subtraction from it.	23 51-55
Not being bothered about the exams: anxious because there is no feeling of anxiety at all		As long as you feel you are working effectively, there is no problem. If you are not, learning some effective revision and anxiety coping techniques may free you to feel anxiety – and cope with it.	39-60 107-145
How to stop worrying about the amount of work to be done, what others will say		See *Ways of coping with anxiety* and *A self guidance checklist to reduce stress* for a large number of ideas to help you.	109,113

The approaches are aimed at how you think feel and behave. As well as suggestions for how to tackle any problems you may have, the approaches are grouped under five headings

1. Thinking and anxiety
2. Breathing techniques
3. Muscular relaxation
4. Visualisation
5. Other approaches

The muscular and breathing techniques are natural techniques that work on the central nervous system and auxiliary nervous system: the thinking and visualisation techniques give you self-help approaches to extend the control you are able to exercise over yourself.

Ways of coping with anxiety
One or more of the following suggestions may both help you reduce anxiety and work effectively:

- Adopt positive attitudes, making positive statements to yourself.
- Stop thoughts that worry you.
- Know and adapt to situations that cause you both the most and the least anxiety.
- Rehearse and simulate situations you find difficult.
- Involve yourself in those activities which reduce anxiety.
- Learn and practise techniques for coping with maximum anxiety, eg panic.
- Learn skills of revising and taking examinations, eg how to set yourself manageable tasks and accomplish them within time limits.
- Learn relaxation techniques.
- Develop a balanced lifestyle.
- Ensure your need for sleep, appropriate diet, company, exercise and variety are met.
- Focus on tasks rather than yourself.
- Have a system for approaching problems and tasks.
- Write things down on paper rather than keeping them in your head.
- Form written hierarchies of difficulty, eg levels of anxiety; topics to be revised.
- Use others as helpers.
- Find our more about other helpful approaches, eg yoga, hypnosis.

Describing your past experience of examinations

It may help you pinpoint your past difficulties to answer these questions, either in the space provided or on a separate piece of paper:

What has been your past experience of tests or exams? What kind of difficulties have you encountered?

Write down as many statements about yourself as possible which relate to any anxieties you have about taking examinations. It may help you to be specific by describing:

what you *thought*, eg 'I've not done enough work.'

what you *felt*, eg very nervous; panic.

how you *behaved*, eg I got stomach aches, couldn't settle down to revision; lost sleep.

Talking over the problem

Having completed answering these questions, you may wish to talk over some issues with a helper. For suggestions see **Using Other as Helpers**. You can also use the **Contents** and **Checklists** to seek answers to the problems you wish to overcome. You may, however, be feeling unclear about what problem to tackle or how to set about it, in which case the next exercise may help you clarify what you will do.

Tackling the problem

If you are feeling unclear about how to tackle a problem, the following four point action sequence may help you to get started.

(1) State the *problem* you wish to resolve:
I want to. . . (This should be specific and contain an action verb, eg write, list, run, etc.)

(2) Set a *goal*:
So that . . . (This should be a well-formed goal statement, clear and obtainable, stating what you wish to be like.)

(3) Determine an *approach*
So I'm going to . . .

(4) Have a *plan of action*
How I'm going to do it . . .

Example

(1) *I want to* learn emergency relaxation techniques.

(2) *So that* I'm never going to 'freeze' or panic in an exam again.

(3) *So I'm going to* learn 3 separate techniques, ie an **emergency quick relaxation technique, breathing slowly and deeply,** and **visualising the examination.**

(4) *How I'm going to do it* is to read the exercises, practise them by myself and then ask a friend to help me rehearse and practise them.

You can use a sheet of paper and the same sentence beginnings, 'I want to . . .' etc, to construct your own action sequence, following the format above.

Drawing up a hierarchy of your anxiety

It may help you to understand more clearly the causes of your anxiety to complete this exercise. Having done so, it will give you guidelines for which part of your anxiety to tackle first and subsequently.

Try to be specific and detailed, sub-dividing the situations if they have a different scale of anxiety, eg 'Entering the Examination room' may sub-divide into – meeting friends waiting outside; finding my seat; waiting for the invigilator to give instructions; turning over the question paper.

You may wish to use the space below or a separate sheet of paper.

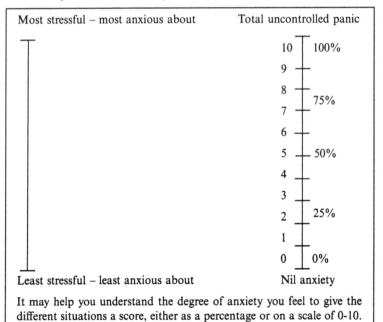

Most stressful – most anxious about	Total uncontrolled panic
	10 100%
	9
	8 75%
	7
	6
	5 50%
	4
	3
	2 25%
	1
	0 0%
Least stressful – least anxious about	Nil anxiety

It may help you understand the degree of anxiety you feel to give the different situations a score, either as a percentage or on a scale of 0-10.

How to use the completed list
You have several choices. You will probably find it easiest to start with situations at the 'least stressful' end of your list, particularly if they have a low anxiety score. You can then adopt one of two approaches.

- Familiarise yourself thoroughly with that situation, simulating, ie recreating as closely as possible, the situation that actually causes you stress, eg sitting at a desk in exam conditions; walking to the exam room; writing timed answers.

- Use one of the relaxation techniques, eg **A do it yourself guide to muscular relaxation**. Once you are in a state of complete relaxation, visualise the least stressful situation as vividly as possible. If you feel any anxiety or any tensing of muscles, then stop and return yourself to a complete state of relaxation again. If this happens at the beginning it means you have not sufficiently sub-divided your least stressful situation – you need a less stressful situation as a starting point.

Generally, you will not feel any tension as you visualise the first, least stressful situation. Having completed it, move on to visualising the second least stressful situation, and so on through your list. If at any point you feel tension you must:

- Stop and return yourself to a state of total relaxation.
- Check to see if your list needs further sub-division; if there is a smaller anxiety step you can take. You will find you can take 2 or 3 steps at a time if this is going well. Don't rush it. Enjoy the state of relaxation and the gradual reduction of anxiety.
- You may find it helpful to use a friend as a helper with this exercise.
- You will no longer feel anxious about those situations you have visualised whilst in a state of complete relaxation.

Learn and practise the exercises designed to cope with your most extreme anxiety, eg **An emergency quick relaxation technique, Breathing slowly and deeply**.

Use the **Contents, Checklist**, your own questions, **The importance of asking questions**, and **Tackling the problem** to help you proceed with other anxiety items on your list.

THINKING AND ANXIETY

A self-guidance checklist to reduce stress

How to use this checklist

1. Read through the whole page, noting points on the left-hand side that apply to you.

2. Ensure you understand the list by checking any of the Notes for guidance that follow.

3. Select 1, 2 or 3 points on the right-hand side that you can start to emphasise immediately, shifting the emphasis of your thinking from the left to the right-hand side.

4. Note other points of relevance on the page. You may return to these on another occasion. Add this approach to any others you have for coping with anxiety.

You are *MORE* likely to feel anxious when you think:	You are *LESS* likely to feel anxious when you think:	Tick (✓) the thinking approaches you will now take:
* about the PAST	about the PRESENT, here and now	
* about the FUTURE, especially the long term future	about here and now, about the VERY NEXT THING YOU DO	
* NEGATIVE self-statements	POSITIVE self-statements	
* about YOURSELF	about TASKS: things you can achieve today	
* about WIDER or LARGER issues, concerns or tasks	about SPECIFIC issues, concerns or tasks	
* of SATISFYING others e.g. what other people will say	of SATISFYING yourself	
* about things YOU CANNOT DIRECTLY AFFECT even if you try	about things YOU CAN DIRECTLY AFFECT if you try	
* that you are UNABLE TO STOP YOURSELF THINKING ABOUT A CONCERN	that you are ABLE TO STOP YOURSELF THINKING ABOUT A PARTICULAR CONCERN	
* you are UNPREPARED	you are PREPARED	
* POSTPONE thinking or doing anything	you are going to take IMMEDIATE APPROPRIATE ACTION	

Notes to guide you about thinking and anxiety

These notes accompany **Thinking and anxiety: a self-guidance checklist to reduce stress**. They explain why certain patterns of thinking are less likely to cause you to feel stressed.

- You cannot do anything about the past. Worrying about a problem, difficulty or failure in the past gives it too great an emphasis in the PRESENT. You can do something about now.

- Thinking about the long-term failure can often feel daunting, even overwhelming. Thinking 'What would happen to me if I fail' fuels anxiety and is counter-productive to success. Planning the short-term future, the VERY NEXT THING YOU DO, the next fifteen minutes, hour, evening, day, week, provides a useful manageable structure.

- Thinking about yourself; how you are feeling, how worried you are, your health, your career prospects, is one of the commonest forms of self-produced stress when studying. The need, when revising for and taking exams, is for you to be able to focus yourself effectively on TASKS, particularly those that are manageable and can be tackled immediately. The **Organising Your Revision** section of the book is packed with suggestions as to how to do this effectively.

- The explanation for avoiding negative self-statements is contained in **Turning negative self-statements into positive self-statements.**

- When you say to yourself, 'I must work tonight' or 'I've got to get some revision done', you are likely to feel overwhelmed. Being highly SPECIFIC about issues, concerns or tasks gives you a manageable routine of activities. An example of an appropriate specific self-statement would be: 'I am going to make a revision card on topic X, test myself on it during the next 30 minutes or so. I'll then make myself a drink and listen to one side of an LP before I tackle the next topic Y in the same way.'

- Even though we can often be more demanding of ourselves than others would be, it is generally more stressful to be thinking about what others expect of you, what they would say if you didn't get the grades or failed, etc. Fear of letting others down is a common form of exam anxiety and an enormous waste of emotional energy. SATISFYING YOURSELF and your own standards is a productive use of your energy.

- You cannot directly affect the examination system, the form it takes, the efficiency or justice of it or when you will take your examinations. Thinking about these is likely to leave you feeling out of control and relatively powerless. You can DIRECTLY AFFECT dozens of things about your life and study – this book is packed with suggestions of what and how – and these are going to help you feel more powerful and resourceful.

- If you are unable to stop yourself thinking about a concern it will certainly fuel your stress. You are ABLE TO STOP YOURSELF THINKING ABOUT A PARTICULAR CONCERN. Use **Turning negative self-statements into positive self-statements** as well as this self-guidance note to aid this process (p 116).

- If you are unprepared – don't know how to revise, have few stress coping techniques and don't know much about the examination procedure – you are certainly more likely to be stressed. You are doing something positive to be PREPARED by reading and using parts of this book.

- Postponing thinking about or doing something invariably fuels anxiety, increasing the intensity, occupying emotional energy unproductively. Taking IMMEDIATE APPROPRIATE ACTION like you are now by using this book is going to relieve these feelings.

Stopping negative thoughts

If you are having thoughts that worry you, try to say consistently to yourself 'Stop' – you may wish to choose another *command word* that has more meaning to you, eg your surname 'Acres!' or something positive 'Think positive' – as soon as you are aware of beginning to think or feel in a particular way. You can add to this some physical movement, like a click of your fingers to reinforce this command to yourself. You must be totally consistent if you adopt this approach. It may be hard work for the first day or so, but after that it will become a habit. This technique is usefully combined with **Turning negative self-statements into positive self-statements**, ie saying 'Stop' to yourself is followed by some positive statement about yourself, your intentions or your success to date.

You can see the usefulness of thought stopping when you feel panic coming on. It is demonstrated in **An emergency quick relaxation technique** (p 128).

Turning negative self-statements into positive self-statements
Stress is often maintained by identifiable negative self-statements. Below in the left-hand column are examples of negative self-statements. In the right-hand column are examples of positive self-statements designed to replace them. Try to identify your own negative self-statements and write them in the blank spaces in the left-hand column. Then, using the positive examples above as a guideline, construct your own positive self-statements. Abandon all negative self-statements and put your energy into positive self-statements.

NEGATIVE STATEMENTS	POSITIVE STATEMENTS
I can't concentrate.	My concentration has really improved. Even when it lapses I know how to recover it.
I can't cope.	I can cope and I'm going to do so.
Everyone seems to be doing more work than I am.	Other people are irrelevant – it's the quality of my learning that matters and I now have the techniques to do my work well.
I might fail. I am going to fail. What if I fail . . .? I won't be able to face 'X' again . . .	I intend to pass, I'm doing a lot to ensure that happens and I can only do my best. That's what I intend to do.
I'm in a mess with my revision. I'll never be able to do enough or catch up. I don't know where to start.	I can get my work done in time when I plan a proper *revision timetable, decide priorities* and know *how to revise* efficiently.
I always make a mess of exams. I've never been able to do well at exams.	The past is irrelevant. I'm now working well and have learnt the techniques to do well in these exams — a new beginning.

Managing exam nerves: self-statements to help you cope
One way of managing your 'nerves', that is your anxiety or even panic, is to learn by heart some statements to help you cope. In the following four situations choose those statements which you can say convincingly to yourself either silently or out loud. At first, you may find it difficult to say any statement convincingly to yourself. In which case, follow this sequence:

- Choose one of two from the existing list *or* add your own.

- Make the statement *real* and realistic to you. Alter it so it remains positive but feels like something you could say to yourself.

- Practise saying it to yourself, regularly. You are aiming for it to become a well ingrained habit to say these statements to yourself rather than the old negative, worrying statements.

- Once you have mastered one or two, add others, expanding your list of useful self-statements, following the same system as above.

The self-statements
Other action you can take is in brackets.

1. Preparing for my exams.
What is it I have to do? (Extract all the parts for you from the examination techniques and anxiety coping sections of this book.)
I'm going to plan what to do about my anxiety and not waste time being anxious.
I'm going to think positively – no negative self-statements. (See other ideas in **Thinking and anxiety: a self-guidance checklist to reduce stress.)**
I'm not going to get involved in conversations I don't want. (Keep conversations that may be anxiety-provoking brief and manageable.)
I'm going to be ready for anything that happens to me.
If the worst happens I'm not going to be thrown into a panic – I'll learn how to cope. (See, for example, **An emergency quick relaxation technique**, p 128).
It will be different this time, I know how to cope.

2. During the exam itself
Now's my chance to put into action what I've learned.
Stick to the here-and-now.
What is the very next thing I'm going to do?
It's different this time – I know how to cope.
I can handle me *and* the tasks.
I can reason and/or relax my fear away.
I need some anxiety: I'll make what I feel work *for* me. (You do! It's a stimulus to coping, awareness, etc.)
Relax, I'm in control. Take a slow, deep breath.
Great. This gives me the chance to show what I know, think, believe, understand, can do, etc.

3. Coping with the feeling of being overwhelmed
Stop! I can manage this panic: it's no different from any other situation
– use the exercises!
When fear comes, just pause.
Stick to here-and-now: What is the very next thing I'm going to do?
I could expect my fear to rise at times. Don't try to eliminate the fear,
just keep it manageable.
Label my fear from 0 to 10 and watch it change.

4. Looking back on the experience
What an achievement.
There'll always be something I could have done better but I've really
done well.
It's a great feeling.
I'm really making progress.
I managed my fear.
It wasn't as bad as I expected.
I've done it.
Wait until I tell . . . (fill in the name of someone important you'd really
want to tell.)

Quotes for yourself
'May you
    Rise in tranquillity
    Walk in peace
    Stay in harmony.'

This is one of my favourite quotes, a Sanskrit saying which I hear at
the end of yoga classes. It creates a feeling of calm and well being.
    There are many others from which you can derive pleasure and good
feelings. If you can find a quotation which helps you have a helpful
perspective on life and exams; keep it with you, or pin it up in front of
you where you study.
    It is particularly helpful to find a phrase which helps you reaffirm a
sense of yourself and a sense of well being. Said to yourself in a moment
of potential or real stress, it can stop any feelings of overwhelmedness. I
have known students change their perception of exams expressing
complete surprise at being able to look forward to a group of exams,
instead of being very frightened of them. There are other ideas in this
section, particularly concerned with visualising and using all your
senses, which can help you change your perceptions around too.

SITUATIONS AND STRESS

How you think, feel or behave can be reinforced by being back in the same immediate environment, in the same place or same situation, eg being in the same room, house, library or with the same people around you.

Here are approaches you can take to cope with stress related to situations.

- *For situations that cannot be avoided* and yet cause you to feel stressed, learn and practise the relaxation ideas in this section. You can come to feel better feelings about people and places by adopting a calmer, more positive, more relaxed approach.

  Where your anxiety is related to unknown or unfamiliar situations, eg the exam room, then try to simulate the situation as closely as possible, eg if your anxiety is about where you are going to take the exam, then find the room in advance, enter it when you are able to do so, get the feel of being in it in a quiet atmosphere. (See also **Getting used to examinations.**)

- *Avoid those situations that cause you stress that are avoidable.* Identify the situations you find stressful. You may wish to list them below or on a separate sheet of paper.

  > Situations I find stressful

Once identified you may wish to use a helper to talk over what you could do to avoid or minimise the stress involved in these situations. **Tackling the problem** may also be a useful aid.

- *Alter what you are doing in these situations* to minimise the stress. For example, if where you are revising is causing you stress, you may be able to improve the furniture arrangement. Moving a piece of furniture so that you get a better view, more natural daylight or enough heat is one approach. Arranging books, files, papers, pens and equipment so that they are accessible around you would be another approach.

- Make a point of *placing yourself in those situations that make you feel good*, relaxed, purposeful, as often as you are able to do so. You may wish to list them below or on a separate sheet of paper. See also **Find a retreat or sanctuary**.

Situations in which I feel good

- *Vary* where you are and who you are with to give yourself the stimulus of a change in environment. Although establishing an effective routine can help both to complete tasks and to work in a composed and effective manner, it may at times leave you feeling unstimulated, bored, jaded.

- *Balancing* a day, or a week or a weekend between tasks, places, people, work, recreation, exercise, diet, sleep and entertainment is a very important skill in maximising the effectiveness of your study.

Find a retreat or sanctuary

A retreat may be outdoors or inside a building. It is a place that feels quiet and where even if there is noise it does not disturb or affect your stillness or focus. In this place you can compose yourself and feel composed.

It may be an actual place such as an old barn in the countryside or the side of a stream which flows into the sea – two real examples of people's sanctuaries. It may be inside a building such as the corner of a public library. The place may not even be quiet. I started to write this idea on a train journey and wrote 'it feels like a quiet place even though there are the sounds of people and the train's movement . . .' I am completing this writing in a college study bedroom listening to Mozart on a Walkman whilst attending a conference. This too feels like a sanctuary even though it's a strange room in a previously unknown place.

In other words, you can carry around your sanctuary with you. Even in unfamiliar places you can organise your environment by sitting at a desk with papers organised around you, your favourite pen in your hand, and perhaps listening to music which soothes and aids your concentration.

You can also organise your inner world as well as your immediate environment. You can take yourself inside yourself to be in touch with feelings of composure experienced elsewhere. There is also the opportunity to *create a scene in the imagination* which may not bear any resemblance to an actual place but which will produce powerful feelings of well being.

WAKING UP IN THE MORNING

There are times during revision when you can feel jaded when waking. Apart from washing and showering, these ideas may help.

Putting your best feet forward

When the ideas of a *Paddle in cold water* and a *Bare foot walk* appeared in the first edition of this book, they received much media attention of the 'Ho . . . Ho . . . Ho . . .' variety. Steve Wright on BBC Radio One poked fun at the idea of cold water paddling; an International news agency in San Diego phoned this loony in England who had this weird idea, and so on. These are the two ideas, repeated as in the original.

Paddle in cold water. Walking up and down in 1 or 2 inches of water in a bath for a minute to two. Not as painful as a cold shower but refreshing, stimulating!

Bare foot walk. A walk in bare feet on paving stones or grass, even with the dew rising, for a few minutes. Walk slowly, steadily, feeling the ground under your feet. This is refreshing and stimulating.

Their principles are simple. Water is a reviver. If you are tired, cold water is likely to revive you. For years, I have used this principle to run some cold water from the shower head onto my feet before it warms up to the temperature I want my shower to be. It helps to wake me up.

And half the world's population start their day in bare feet, walking on the bare earth – whether by choice or not. There is real advantage in bare feet for 'earthing' or 'grounding' yourself and setting yourself up for the new day. It is not always possible or desirable to do it in colder climates – it is not the top of everyone's preferences on cold winter mornings in England! It fits better in the summer.

Other approaches

Physical exercise

A jog, run, brisk walk or swim are all potentially stimulating at the beginning of a day. Your circulation can equally well be stimulated by stepping up on a chair, and stepping down again, between 5 and 10 times, or any similar exercises, such as those contained in the Canadian Air Forces XBX exercises. All these physical pursuits need to be appropriate to your health, fitness and age to aid your alertness rather than decrease it!

The complete breath
This is a version of the simple yoga exercise, described in Richard Hittleman's useful book, *Yoga for Health*. It is included in **Breathing techniques** (p 128).

Drink water
One simple technique for picking up your energy level is to drink water. If you energy feels low, pause, sit still and sip some water until you feel 'revived' to tackle the next stage of your learning.

There is a tendency among many students to drink too little water during periods of intense study. Hot stimulant drinks such as coffee do not have the same benefit as pure water, although they may raise your adrenalin in a different way.

The morning before an afternoon exam

- Prepare a free morning before an afternoon exam in advance. By the evening before, know how you are going to spend the time, dividing it into half an hour and, if appropriate, quarter of an hour units.
- Plan into the morning some relaxation, exercise or quiet, low key entertainment, eg listening to music.
- *Don't attempt any new revision topics* – Attempting to learn *new* topics at this late stage can affect your recall of those topics you already know and/or understand well.
- Use any key word cards or notes you have, not great bulky files, simply to recall and re-check your understanding, asking questions to which you will provide answers, without looking at the card. This simulates the exam conditions.
- For a paper involving mathematics or problem solving, practise your recall of methods or formulae for more familiar questions.
- Plan into the morning when and what you are going to eat and drink. Try to eat something of nutritional value, but watch your liquid intake – many exams are 2 or 3 hours long!
- Incorporate all the relevant ideas from **On the way to the exam.**

On the way to the exam

You will maximise your effectiveness in examinations if you organise the time immediately before an examination. It will also enable you to minimise your anxiety. Some or all of the following ideas will also help.

- Minimise your waiting time outside an exam room, know the location of the room and time your walk, rehearsing it if necessary.

You may either come direct from your home or find a temporary waiting place, near the exam room that you can use until a few minutes before the examination.

- Meet only those people you want to meet, if any. Agree with friends not to stand around before the exam making anxiety-provoking conversation, eg about how nervous you are feeling; what topics you have revised or questions you think are going to be on the paper. Avoid waiting around outside altogether or talking to anybody, if you wish, by timing your arrival so that you can walk straight into the room a few minutes before the exam is due to start.
- Practise your rehearsed self-statements. Keep them positive. You are ready to go.
- Practise your breathing, visualising, muscular and/or **Emergency Quick Relaxation** techniques both to keep your composure and as practice in the event of their being needed (p 128).

Getting to sleep at night
If you are finding it hard to fall asleep at night or are waking early, there are several approaches you can take. Select those which have most appeal to you, are most available and possible.

Causes of sleep loss
A first approach is to *cope with any anxiety* you are feeling *about the disrupted sleep pattern.* You can almost certainly lose sleep for short periods of time without the loss having a profound effect upon you. Some of the anxiety coping techniques in this section of the book can be used to help you cope with any such anxiety.

You may, of course, be deliberately cutting down on sleep to cram in more revision and study time. You can keep a check on whether this sleep loss is adversely affecting your study effectiveness by self-monitoring.

Ask yourself:
  – Are you being agitated, upset or angered by small incidents?
  – Is your concentration noticeably deteriorating, both by 'not being able to take anything in' or not being able to recall something you have just read or done?
  – Are you feeling emotionally overwhelmed by all the tasks?
  – Do you lack energy and/or appetite?

If the answer to some of these questions is 'yes', then it is likely that your need for sleep (or proper diet, exercise, company, entertainment or relaxation, which are also considered in this section of the book) is not being met.

Ideas to help you sleep at night

Watch what you eat and drink
Avoid indigestible food, excessive liquid and stimulants such as cola, hot chocolate, or too much coffee. Alcohol needs to be monitored as well. Whilst a small quantity can act as a relaxant and decrease your alertness, large quantities will act as a depressant and reduce your ability to achieve or rest easily.

Take exercise
Walks, jogs, runs, swims, a game of squash, an exercise programme, are all familiar, appropriate examples. Being physically tired, even exhausted, does certainly help you sleep. Studying is often a very physically passive business: it needs to be broken up with activity and a change of scenery.

Experience a sense of achievement
If you have completed a task, no matter how small, you are likely to be able to rest easier. Use the techniques in the **Organising Your Revision** section of the book to help with this.

Learn to juggle
Juggling has become particularly popular as a way of relaxing over the last few years. There is a school of thought which says that in order to manage the stress and strains of study, everyone can do something 'mindless' for five minutes every day, that is, something which requires no conscious thought. Juggling is a very good example of a meditative technique which becomes relaxing as you begin to develop a little confidence and competence in it.

Exercises and postures
Use relaxation exercises or postures, illustrated and explained in this book. Practise them working at a good, relaxed, sleeping posture. See **A good sleeping posture.**

Recall the day – in reverse
When in a relaxed sleep posture, try, as an alternative to counting sheep, recalling the events of the day moment-by-moment in detail. However, do it backwards, ie starting from the very last thing you did before you got into bed. Hopefully you won't get as far as recalling when you woke up.

Meet your need for entertainment
Meet your need for entertainment, for a break from study. Think about

what causes you to enjoy yourself, relax and take your mind fully away
from study. The list of possible activities is endless. The following are
some examples students have mentioned to me during the course of
one term: playing a guitar, listening to music on headphones, writing
songs and poems, watching films, taking photographs, going to discos,
going to the pub, cooking a meal for friends.

Enjoy the close company of others
A close friendship or friendships involving the ability to share
intimacies, be open, being yourself is immensely valuable at any time
and particularly at times of pressure.

Use water
Water is very therapeutic. Warm baths or showers can be excellent
relaxants immediately before going to bed, as can swimming.

Saunas and massage
If you have access to a sauna or know anybody who can offer a skilled
massage, both are excellent relaxants prior to sleep.

Go to bed at a time you are ready for sleep
You may be familiar with the idea of 'biological clocks', that
everybody has a natural rhythm, a sequence of ups and downs
(cycles) that affect their alertness, need for sleep, mood and other
aspects of their being. Whether or not you understand or accept the
idea, there seems to me to be no doubt that there are differences in both
the amount of sleep people need and the time they need to go to sleep.

My experience is that some people need to get to bed early after
completing their study in the early evening, whilst others can work very
effectively late at night, studying to midnight and beyond. In general,
those in early or mid-teens seem less able to study late into the night
than those in late teens or older age groups, but there will be
exceptions. If you have developed an effective means of self-monitoring
yourself, you can prevent yourself from attempting to work beyond
your productive limits. Try to be honest with yourself. If you know it is
your anxiety that is keeping you up and your concentration,
understanding and retention is poor, you are wasting time that could
be valuably used the next day for study.

Likewise, there is no point in going to bed to try to sleep when you
don't feel like sleep. Use the time more constructively, more creatively
(as suggested above). Further, there seems little point in lying in bed
worrying about not sleeping. You would be better occupied doing
something which caused you less stress: making yourself a drink;

listening to music on headphones; tackling a small, yet niggling, study task; using one of the relaxation exercises.

Finding someone to talk to
Seek out those people to whom you can talk with confidence. Those who will listen attentively, not moralise, keep confidentiality and help yourself to put things in perspective. Take this book along. Use it together, selecting the ideas which best suit you.

And if you still aren't sleeping . . .
If your lack of sleep continues it may be advisable to visit your doctor. There is no clear cut guideline on how long you should tolerate disruption of sleep before seeking help, although between one and three weeks would seem appropriate.

Developing a good sleeping posture
A good sleeping posture is illustrated below. Lie on your right side, drawing up your bent left leg so that it comes comfortably to rest alongside your waist area. Your right leg stretches out straight.

Allow your right arm to lie straight alongside your right side, whilst your left arm is bent. Your head should be supported by a pillow or pillows.

You may prefer to try this on your left side or make small alterations to the position of your arms and legs.

A good sleeping posture

A total relaxation position when lying down

The corpse
The objective of the 'corpse' is to be able to completely relax every muscle in your face and body. Anxiety will lessen when you relax muscles.

It involves lying on the floor, a bed, in or on a sleeping bag, pillows or cushions and is a position that encourages deep relaxation and sleep. Wear comfortable, loose clothing and dispense with shoes.

• Lie down slowly on your back with your arms by your sides.
• Allow your arms to come to rest with your hands a few inches away from your body and palms upwards, curling your fingers if they want to do so.
• Your feet should be allowed to fall open, spreading outwards, until they settle in a comfortable position a few inches apart.
• Raise your chin 6 to 8 cm (2 inches or so), tilting your head backwards so that your eyes are facing directly above you, then close your eyes.
• Try to let all your muscles become limp and heavy. Let your facial muscles go, your arms and legs become floppy and heavy, settling into a comfortable, still posture.
• Inhale deeply and slowly to enable your whole breathing to slow down with each intake of breath, don't take another breath until you have to do so. Simply concentrate your attention on your breathing and nothing else.
• You may stay in this position for any length of time. When you have finished, rise very slowly to avoid dizziness, raising yourself into a sitting or semi-upright position on your right side before eventually standing.

A total relaxation position when lying down
Initially, lie as in the position for the Corpse. There are two differences as you can see in the illustration. The first is that you raise your knees, so that they are firmly and comfortably supported by your feet on the ground. The knees should be between approximately 12 cm and 30 cm (6 to 12 inches) apart.

The second difference is that you raise your head 5 to 8 cm (2 to 3 inches) by resting the back on a thick book or books or a cushion. As with the corpse, raise your chin by tilting your head back 5 cm (2 inches) or so.

You may then close your eyes, breathing slowly and deeply as in the Corpse.

As with the Corpse you may continue in the position which enables the base of your spine to be very comfortably supported, as long as you wish or time permits. Rise, as in all such exercises, very slowly, sitting up first then slowly rising to your feet.

This is a lovely relaxing position, for a few minutes or a longer period of time.

The cat nap

Closing your eyes for a few minutes can be extremely valuable at times of pressure. Twenty minutes sleep, lying down, sitting on a comfortable chair or sofa can be immensely refreshing and enable you to continue your studying for some hours afterwards.

My own favourite is to use the Corpse, laying on the floor or on my bed. I set an alarm clock if I know I do not want to over-sleep but I generally find I stir naturally, using my own time clock. I do not necessarily fall into a deep sleep, but I am conscious of cutting off from full consciousness and enjoying the experience of relaxing physically, as well as emotionally.

BREATHING TECHNIQUES

Learning how to breathe more fully and appropriately by using one or more of these exercises is another very helpful approach to removing tension and refreshing yourself.

An emergency quick relaxation technique

This exercise is to counteract panic and the build up of tension. It is adapted from Jane Madder's useful book *Stress and Relaxation*.

(1) Say sharply to yourself STOP! (aloud if the situation permits).
(2) Breathe in and hold your breath for a moment before *slowly* exhaling. As you do so relax your shoulders and hands. (See also **A do-it-yourself guide to muscular relaxation**).
(3) Pause for a moment, then as you breathe in slowly again, relax your forehead and jaw.
(4) Stay quiet for a few moments then go on with what you were doing, moving slowly and smoothly.
(5) If you have to talk, speak a little more slowly and with your voice a little lower than usual.

This STOP! relaxation can usually be done without anybody noticing and you will find that, in spite of your feelings, the tension will lessen.

The complete breath

The essential feature of this exercise is that everything is completed SLOWLY.

(1) Stand upright with your arms by your side. Exhale (see figure 1).
(2) Breathe in through your nose. As you do so, inhale, filling as fully as possible your stomach/abdomen area first and thereafter your chest (see figure 2).
(3) At the same time, bring your arms above your head and rise on to your toes.
    Hold this for a moment (see figure 3).
(4) Breathe out through your nose, expelling the air from your abdomen through your chest. As you do so, lower your arms to your sides and your feet to the floor again.

You can repeat this between 3 and 10 times. If you wish you can count to 8 as you inhale and do the same as you exhale. Alternatively, you can start to raise yourself onto the balls of your feet when your arms reach the horizontal halfway point of their journey to above your head, lowering yourself onto your heels slowly from the halfway point of their journey down.

Breathing slowly and deeply

The same sequence illustrated in the **The complete breath** can be used at any time, without the accompanying stretching movements. It is useful to avoid the build up of tension, or to reduce it once it has occurred.

The sequence is as follows:

(1) Breathe in slowly through your nose to the count of 8. As you inhale the air, imagine you are filling your stomach/abdomen area first and thereafter your chest.
(2) Hold this breath in for as long as it remains comfortable to do so.
(3) Expel the air slowly through your nose to the count of 8, expelling the air from your abdomen upwards through your chest.
(4) Refrain from taking another intake of breath until it becomes uncomfortable and repeat the sequence 1 to 4, again.

Three times is usually enough to reduce the level of tension and to refresh you. You may extend this if you need to do so. It is a useful technique for the exam room.

Alternate nostril breathing
This is an effective relaxant that can help with tension and head congestion.

Inhale through the right nostril, closing the left nostril with the thumb of your left hand. Count slowly to 4 as you inhale.

Close both nostrils with your left thumb and forefinger and hold your breath to the slow count of 4.

Exhale through your left nostril to the slow count of 4, whilst closing your right nostril with your forefinger (or first two fingers whichever you find easier).

Release both nostrils, remaining without breath for another count of 4.

Repeat, breathing in through the left nostril.

Once you have established an even 4-4-4-4 routine and can complete the thumb and forefinger movements easily, close your eyes when doing this exercise.

You can try variations on this 4-4-4-4 routine. Try *in* for 6, count to 3; *out* for 6, count to 3; *in* for 6, etc. 8/4/8/4 combinations, once you're used to the others, will slow and deepen your breathing even more. You can practise this exercise for 5 minutes or so at a time – even three or four sequences will be beneficial.

Breathing at three levels
There are three levels of breathing which you can come to detect well if you practise yoga techniques.

Level one
When you are anxious your breathing is often shallow. If you locate where you are breathing it is at the top of the chest. You will probably

find you are breathing quite quickly. If asked to speak your voice is likely to tremble and be quite quiet with this level of breathing.

Level two
This is deeper breathing which comes to and from the chest. You are likely to feel less anxious, have a stronger voice when asked to speak in a public situation and breathe more slowly than in level one. Much of your breathing in everyday life is likely to be in level two (or fluctuating between level one and level two).

Level three
When you take a full, deep, intake of breath you move into level three breathing. What happens is that your diaphragm moves down to create a vacuum in the lung cavity and pushes out the abdomen. You can see and feel your stomach filling up and emptying. You could imagine yourself filling up a balloon on the in-breath. If you gently lay your hand on your stomach you will feel it rise and fall. The higher you go the better as it means that you are drawing in air to fill the lungs. Do not overstrain though.

Breathe through the nose whenever possible and breathe out through the nose as well.

Your out-breath should be more emphasised than the in-breath and take a little longer. If you sigh slightly as you release the breath, you will find it will help to release tension.

Similarly, if you tense and then relax your shoulders by allowing them to drop with a sigh, you will be helping to let go of your tension.

You can also hold your breath at the end of the exhalation, for 2 to 5 seconds, to enable yourself to be still before a full inhalation begins.

As with other exercises in breathing you need only repeat it five times in order to feel the benefit of this deep breathing exercise, which you can do in a sitting position. Over time it will generate a feeling of well being.

MUSCULAR RELAXATION

The basic principle involved in muscular relaxation is that when muscles are tensed really hard and then relaxed, the muscles will go into a deeper state of relaxation than formerly. When your muscles are relaxed in this way *you cannot be in a state of tension* – the two states are not compatible. In such a composed physical state you are going to be able to study more effectively, and be mentally alert with the negative effects of anxiety behind you.

You can achieve muscular relaxation as an after-effect from strenuous physical exertion such as running, squash, swimming, squat thrusts and team ball games. Such exertion will cause you to breathe more deeply and fully and this will also contribute to your more relaxed state afterwards. There are obvious differences in fitness and overall health that determine what exercise is appropriate to you; how much exercise; how often and for how long. A marathon run is not generally an appropriate starting point of most people! Physical Education teachers, the Health Education Council's 'Look after Yourself' materials and courses as well as medical opinion are all available for you to consult if you are in doubt about what is appropriate for you.

In addition, the following exercises will give you practice of muscular relaxation.

- a do it yourself guide to muscular relaxation
- exercises to use when sitting at a desk
- an exercise for relaxing your head and neck
- sit and relax
- touch that helps – hugs and cuddles
- the touch that brings well being.

A do it yourself guide to muscular relaxation
Relaxation of individual muscle groups or the whole body is a skill which everyone can learn and which improves with practice. It is important to be able to recognise muscle tension and then to release this tension at will. It is only when this skill has been learned that the full benefits of muscular relaxation during anxious and stressful situations can be achieved.

The following programme involves tensing and then relaxing the main muscle groups of the body in turn. Ideally, each group should be tensed and the tension released three times in succession:
   first of all tensing the muscles as tightly as possible
   secondly with moderate tension
   finally with minimal tension
It may help you to count to 5 slowly and silently on each of these three tensings. This helps us to recognise the muscle tension which is part of our reaction to stress, and the contrasting feel of muscles which are relaxed.

The best way to learn the skill of relaxation is to find a friend who will slowly talk you through the programme on pages 133-134. If this is not possible, read through the programme and learn the order of muscles to be relaxed and then work through from memory or from a key word card

Time required
At first it will take approximately 20 to 30 minutes to go through the

Your relaxation programme

Part of the body (key words)	Instructions (repeat each movement three times)	What you will feel (helpers read this aloud after the instructions)
Start with the face *Forehead* Raise eyebrows	Raise your eyebrows and frown heavily, with maximum tension *Repeat* with moderate and minimal tension	Feel the tension across the forehead and scalp. Release the tension and feel the forehead become smooth and the muscles relax
Eyes and nose Screw up eyes	Screw your eyes up tightly	Feel the tension spreading over the whole of your face and the contrasting calm, soothing feeling as the tension is released
Mouth and jaw Clench teeth	Clench your teeth together firmly to tense the jaw muscles	Feel the tension around the jaw and throat. Release the tension and let your jaw muscles become loose letting your mouth hang open if it wishes
Ear-to-ear grin	Tense the muscles around the mouth by smiling in an exaggerated way – an ear-to-ear grin – then let the smile fade away	Feel the muscles relax
Tongue	Tense the tongue by pressing it firmly against the back of the teeth. Slowly release and let the tongue rest in the mouth	Feel the release of tension and the tongue relaxing in your mouth
Forearms Wrist back – hand forward	Bend your wrist back and push forward hard with your hand	As you let the tension go, feel warm, tingling sensation of relaxed muscles in the forearms
Upper arms Bend elbows	Bend both arms at the elbow. Flex the biceps really firmly, slowly relax these muscles	Feel the heaviness in your arms spread down to your finger tips
Shoulders and chest Hands and arms at side	Press your hands and the arms firmly against the side of your body. Press really hard and then release the tension and let your shoulders hang loose	Your arms will feel heavy and relaxed again

Your relaxation programme

Part of the body (key words)	Instructions (repeat each movement three times)	What you will feel (helpers read this aloud after the instructions)
Neck and back Chin out	Jut your chin out in front of you or, if you are lying down, raise your head about one inch from the ground	Feel the tension in your neck muscles and its release as you bring your head down to a comfortable resting position
Chin in	Draw your chin in towards your neck or, if lying down, press your head back into the floor. Hold it briefly, then release	Feel tension building in your neck, shoulders and back Enjoy the contrasting feel of the muscles as they relax and lose the tension
Neck stretch	Elongate your neck and feel the tension until it is released	Feel the tension until it is released and slowly subsides
Retract neck	Retract your neck by shortening your neck as much as possible	Feel the tension and slowly release it
Shrug shoulders	Try and touch your ears with your shoulders then let them slump back	Feel a heavy relaxed feeling once more which is spreading through your upper body
Shoulder blades	Draw your shoulder blades firmly together	Feel the tightness created then relax the muscles and let your shoulders slump
Arched back	Hollow your back by arching it more and more. Relax back into chair or on to the floor	Feel the support that the chair or floor offers
Stomach, thighs and buttocks Pull in stomach	Pull your stomach muscles in tighter and tighter, then let go	Feel warmth and tingling feelings as it is released
Heels against floor	With feet flat on the floor, pull the heels backwards against the resistance of the floor, tightening all the muscles at the back of the thighs. Relax these muscles. With feet still flat on the floor press the heels down firmly into the floor and let the muscles relax completely	Feel the difference when the tension is released
Buttocks	Tighten muscles in your buttocks and release	Feel the release of tension that this produces
Calves and feet Point toes	Point your toes, extending the ankle joint. Then let the ankle become loose and the muscles relaxed	Feel the tension in the muscles at the back of the lower leg
Toes up	Flex the ankle by bending the toes up towards the knee	Feel the tension build again. Feel the warm, tingling feeling of relaxation spread down your legs
Curl toes	Curl your toes up tightly then release this tension 3 times	With the strain release, let the toes rest naturally
Stretch toes	Stretch your toes out strongly as far as you can	As the feet relax completely let the soothing, heavy feeling in your legs spread to the tips of your toes

entire procedure properly. With practice you will be able to become quite relaxed in 10 to 15 minutes.

An alternative is to buy a commercially produced relaxation programme on audio-tape. More details of some programmes are included in **Further Reading and Help**. Yet another alternative is to record your own audio-tape, using this programme.

Like any other skill (driving a car, playing the piano) it will need practice, but the benefits can be enormous, and it is enjoyable to do in itself!

The relaxation programme

Sit and relax

Just settle back in a chair and find a position where you are comfortable. Let the chair support your body weight. Let your hands rest on your lap and have your head comfortably balanced on your neck and shoulders. (If you prefer, lie down on the floor or on a bed with your legs stretched out. Let your arms lie loosely alongside your body, as in the Corpse, palms turned down, of it is more comfortable

---

A Do It Yourself Guide to Muscular Relaxation

Sequence (Key word   RELAXATION – Muscular

1. Raise eyebrows   N.B. *SLOWLY*

2. Screw up eyes

3. Clench teeth   Tensing – 3 times

4. Ear-to-ear grin   Maximum) tensing to count

5. Tongue   Moderate) of 5

                      Minimum)

             6. Wrist back – hand forward

             7. Bend elbows   *Note* most stressed

             8. Hands and arms at side   muscles. Concentrate on these.

9. Chin out

10. Chin in

11. Neck stretch

12. Retract neck

13. Shrug shoulders

14. Shoulder blades

15. Arched back

             16. Pull in stomach   19. Point toes

             17. Heels against floor   20. Toes up

             18. Buttocks   21. Curl toes

                                    22. Stretch toes

have your hands resting across your abdomen.) Now close your eyes. Sigh to release tension. Pay attention to the rhythm of your own breathing. Breathe out a little more deeply. Feel your abdomen rise as you breathe in and as you exhale feel your whole body sink into the chair, letting all your muscles relax. Pause for a while.

You are now in a state of total relaxation
Concentrate on the rhythm of your own breathing as you sit/lie in total relaxation. Think of all the muscles you have just relaxed and feel them sinking into a deeper state of relaxation. In times of stress, muscle tension can manifest itself in different parts of the body – eg the clenched fist, the furrowed brow, the aching neck and shoulders – so *concentrate particularly on the muscle groups which reflect your anxiety and tension* and register the way they feel in this relaxed state.

Ending the relaxation programme
When you are ready to end this period of relaxation come round very slowly. Just wiggle your toes and fingers a little when you are ready, have a stretch and open your eyes. You should feel refreshed and calm, ready to face the demands of your daily life.

Exercises to use when sitting at a desk during exams or revision
These isometric exercises involve some of the same principles involved in **A do it yourself guide to muscular relaxation.**

Pull in stomach muscles tightly	Grasp below seat of chair
hold for count of 5	pull up for count of 5
Relax	Relax
Clench first tightly	Press elbows tightly into side of body
hold for count of 5	hold for count of 5
Relax	Relax
Extend fingers	Push foot hard into floor
hold for a count of 5	hold for count of 5
Relax	Relax

An exercise for relaxing your head and neck
Allow your head to DROP forward. Try not to pull it down. You should feel muscles at back of your beck being stretched by the weight of your head. Repeat, allowing your head to drop backward, then to the left and right.

A selection of the above exercises will only take about 30 seconds and can be most helpful to relieve the strain (or even cramp) which occurs when sitting writing at a desk during an examination. Performed between questions or sections of an exam, the exercises may also aid in 'switching off' from one topic and focussing on the next.

Touch that helps – hugs and cuddles

In her *Little Book of Hugs*, Katherine Keating's cartoon bears point out the many and varied ways we can both give and receive a hug. Stressful times such as exams are times when we can be enormously supported by human touch and many students have said how important a friend's cuddle or supportive arm around the shoulders has been when they have felt fragile and/or emotionally exhausted.

Visualise being hugged

Even if a safe hug is not available to you during the revision period (and it won't be in the exam room) then you can visualise receiving a hug.

Adopt the usual routine for calming and relaxing yourself by sitting in a comfortable, quiet place. Breathe slowly and deeply four or five times and allow yourself to sink into the chair, feeling the weight of your limbs.

Imagine yourself meeting a good friend, greeting each other with a 'hello' and a smile with you both putting your arms around each other in a gentle but firm, warm embrace. You can use this image for comfort and reassurance by practising it prior to the exams and using the image of it in the exam room if you're feeling the need of some support.

S-l-o-w-l-y does it

Another idea for calming yourself in the exam situation is to focus on the words SLOW and SLOWLY. Picture the word S L O W on a white or blackboard. Say it to yourself, slowly. Breathe in slowly, Hold your breath for a few moments and then let out the breath slowly.

When you slow your breathing down you slow your heart rate down too. You'll leave behind the shallow-breathing, heart-fluttering anxiety-state.

You can use this approach to help you read instructions on exam papers by saying S L O W and S L O W L Y to yourself as you first read, and then follow, the instructions precisely.

The touch that brings well being

Here are three simple ideas you can use to help your own physical well being.

Technique 1

Using the fingertips of both hands, very lightly and gently stroke the surface of your face. Start with your forehead, laying your fingertips in the middle of your brow above your nose, and draw the fingers of both hands gently across your forehead at the same time. Do it slowly and repeat five times.

Then do the same, again using both hands very lightly
– over your eyes and eye sockets (5 times)
– along both sides of your nose, moving downwards (5 times)
– over the remainder of your cheeks, moving sideways (5 times)
– over your cheekbones, downwards to your chin (5 times)
– over your mouth and lips (5 times)
– under your cheek bone and along your neck (5 times)
– from your ears downwards (5 times).

You are likely to feel soothed as a result and the whole process only takes a few minutes.

Technique 2

Use one hand to gently stroke
– your forehead
– the inside of both arms where your elbow bends, ensuring you make skin-to-skin contact. Use both hands to gently stroke both arms.
– use one hand to gently stroke the back of the other, then reverse it.

Do this slowly for as many times as you wish, and as often as you wish. (These three areas of the body have been found to provide maximum comfort to disturbed or upset children with special needs).

Technique 3

In the palm of your hand there is a spot which has been identified for thousands of years as being one of the meridians of the body and to be concerned with mental well being.

It is located about four or five cms below the gap between our second and third fingers. If you feel around with your index finger into the opposite palm as it remains relaxed and facing upward, you will find a small indentation in your palm, into which your finger is able to press. If you have found the right indentation or dip in the hand, when you exert some pressure into that place it will feel a little sensitive, even sore. If it does, you have found the right place.

The idea is to exert some firm but gentle pressure with that one finger on that point, to stimulate a feeling of well being. If you find that a far-fetched idea, you can also combine pressure with a visualisation of some pleasant scene or good experience. In that way you form a link between a discreet (quite well hidden) part of the body and another sensation you like (this is a process known as 'anchoring').

I have shown this technique to students who had a real fear of flying and at least two people were able to use it well, when it was linked into a number of other techniques.

VISUALISATION

Four ways to use visualisation
Creating a picture in your mind or visualisation has at least four uses when studying for exams. Use the same upward eye movements as described in Chapter Four, **Improving your memory**.

Visual memorising
Its use has been explained in remembering and in constructing key word revision cards in the **Organising Your Revision** section.

Using a dream as a goal
At fourteen years of age, Duncan Goodhew, a future swimming champion, determined he was going to go to the Olympics. It was his target, his goal throughout the years of hard training. He imagined how it would be, the race, what it would feel like afterwards and this dream drove him on and sustained him over the years. This use of a dream as a goal is well known to many sportsmen and women. They are aware that it is not just ability, technique, determination or hard work that create success, but an extra key factor within the person. It is not always clear what this is, but a dream is certainly one such factor. Constructing your own dream, visualising what you intend to achieve for yourself, could become a powerful motivating force for you in your study.

Visualise taking the examination
Use one of the relaxation exercises to bring yourself into a composed,

comfortable and relaxed state.

Now imagine yourself in the same composed, calm state taking the examination.

You feel purposeful and confident. You see yourself at a desk, in the exam room environment. You feel entirely at home and attuned to that moment, working effectively and concentrating well.

Practise visualising this positive, clear, realistic image over and over again.

Visualising as a relaxation technique
Create a scene in your imagination and **A wave of relaxation through your body** are two exercises using the visualisation principle, and **Imagining your limbs feeling warm and heavy** is another, using what you have learned about **Muscular relaxation**.

Create a scene in your imagination
The ability to create a scene in your imagination as a place to retreat into when stress is near can be very useful.

- Think of a scene or a moment in time in your mind. It can be real or imaginary; from the past, present or future.
- The essential features of this scene are that it creates within you pleasant feelings of safety, warmth, security, peace.
- It must be unaffected by bad messages, uneasy thoughts, painful memories.
- In your imagination create as vivid a scene as possible. Picture the scene, the colours, the movement in the scene, the precise detail. *Hear* the sounds associated with the scene in the same kind of detail. *Feel* the touch experiences associated with the moment such as temperature; wind; the feel of your body; anything you touched. Add to these any *tastes* or *smells* associated with the moment.
- It may take you a little time to construct such a scene. You may choose to have more than one. Practise recalling this scene several times when not feeling stressed. With practice it can be very quickly brought to mind. It can only take a few seconds, or at most a minute or two, to dwell in this lovely imagined world. You can then quickly return to present reality in a more composed state.

You can use this technique in any situation, eg an exam room, standing around waiting for something to happen. It is not visible to other people, except perhaps by the peaceful look on your face.

In learning it, however, you may find it helpful to sit in a comfortable chair or lie on a bed and use other relaxation exercises such as breathing or muscular relaxation before it.

Three scenes to imagine
You may wish to try to take yourself in your imagination through all three of these scenes or one may well appeal to you more than others.

Scene 1 – The glade
You come upon a sunlit glade in a forest. Move around it long enough to chose the best spot for you to sit or lie in complete comfort. Here is tranquillity, peace and calm. Here you can hear the sound of buzzing insects, smell the scents of the grasses and wild flowers shimmering in the heat whilst you watch the sunlight pushing through the rustling leaves in the trees that are around you.

Scene 2 – The running water
You are sitting by the side of a stream. The spot you have chosen enables you to sit comfortably, perhaps hugging your knees and to watch the stream as it rushes, glides and sparkles past you. You watch the progress of leaves as they whirl by or glide into the stiller waters at the edge of the stream. The sounds of the stream are constantly ringing in your ears and being absorbed into your being. You are aware of the lightest breeze touching your face. Here you can absorb yourself into being at one with the stream of life and the feeling of well being.

Scene 3 – The beach
You are laid on a beautiful beach of golden sand. Ahead of you lies the deep blue ocean with its waves lapping against the sand. Behind and to the side you can see palm trees waving in the cooling breeze. The sky is cloudless and the sun beams down. You are warm, relaxed and full of well being. All is well with your world.

With each of these scenes, count yourself out from them by simply saying '5-4-3-2-1' to yourself and then checking you are focussed on the reality around you but with a composed frame of mind. You may not be able to use any of these three scenes because they fail to appeal to you or because you suffer from hay fever or have a concern about being near water or exposed to the sun. If this is the case, you can *create your own scene in your imagination.*

A wave of relaxation through your body

- Sit comfortably in a chair or lie in a comfortable position.
- Close your eyes and imagine yourself to be transparent and filled with your favourite colour of liquid. Imagine it to be exactly at the temperature you find comfortable. If you are unsure of a colour,

choose some variation of blue, eg turquoise or aquamarine.
- Starting from the crown of your head, imagine this liquid draining slowly away down your body. As it does so, imagine each part of the body from which it has drained feeling lighter and relieved of tension. Imagine the liquid eventually flowing out through the tips of your fingers and toes and you'll be left feeling relaxed. Repeat if necessary. Move only slowly when you first rise, to avoid dizziness.

Imagining your limbs feeling warm and heavy

Once you are aware of how muscles feel when they are relaxed and you have used your imagination to develop a composed state of mind, you can combine these two approaches in this exercise.

Lying down or sitting comfortably, imagine your limbs to be feeling very heavy. It may help you to close your eyes for a while and focus upon one part of the body at a time, eg your right hand; lower arm; upper arm.

Once all the limbs feel heavy, imagine a feeling of warmth in all these limbs. Exclude from this your neck area (where tension is often to be found). Imagine your neck to feel cool and light.

With practice this exercise only takes a few minutes and can be used in an upright sitting posture in the exam room.

Gazing as relaxation

A simple meditative exercise involves gazing at a candle flame. Light a candle and sit a distance of three to five feet or so away from it. Gaze into the heart of it – to the area just above the wick where there appears to be a vacuum in the flame. Minimise the amount of times you blink and two or three minutes of gazing is quite sufficient before you close your eyes. You may well see an after-image of the flame which you can follow behind your eyelids.

Ensuring that you are sitting in a comfortable chair, on a cushion or cross-legged on the floor, you will find this exercise will enhance your concentration and still your mind. You can add to it by playing some baroque music such as Mozart or some of the alternative types of music available from specialist shops and designed as meditative, whole earth or spiritual sounds.

Gazing at movement in water is another major way in which many people relax. Apart from gazing at waves crashing against the seashore or rushing over rocks in a stream, you will find that a number of waiting areas of doctors' and dentists' practices use another therapeutic device – the fish tank.

I have known very distressed people become calm within half an hour of gazing at small fish moving in a tropical fish tank. It is a well-known and successful way of shedding preoccupations, so if you have an opportunity to gaze at one – try it.

Focussed listening

This exercise complements the **Visualise taking the exam** exercise in that it helps focus attention and concentration in the exam room. In addition, it is a relaxation exercise in its own right. The object of the exercise is to develop your ability to listen to only those sounds you wish to hear and thus be more discriminating in your listening. Thus if potentially disruptive sounds occur in or outside the exam room you will continue to maintain your concentration. A window cleaner whistling; a lawn mower working outside (quite a common occurrence this in summer exams); building or road works; another candidate taken ill are examples of situations that you will be able to take in your stride.

The exercise

- Spend around 60 seconds listening to sounds outside the room you are in, eg sounds of traffic, birds, rain or wind, voices, footsteps on stairs.
- Another 60 seconds listening to sounds in the room, eg a radiator clinking, the movement of a chair, a clock ticking, a cough.
- Another 60 seconds listening to the sounds immediately around you and within you eg breathing, the movement of your paper and pen, the sound of clearing your throat, your chair.

It is this third – emphasised – listening that you wish to be able to develop and use in the exam room, excluding the sounds in the room and beyond.

Practise being able to focus on your immediate environment in this way as an aid to your concentration.

OTHER APPROACHES TO MANAGING ANXIETY

It is not only a visit to your GP or a homeopath that can help you manage the balancing of your anxiety and well being. There are a whole range of alternative approaches open to you, a number of which are offered privately on a fee-paying basis more commonly than they are offered as a free service.

Book to see a counsellor

You will probably be able to book an appointment to see a counsellor in most colleges of further and higher education. This will generally be a free service and hardly an 'alternative' health approach as counselling has become a very heavily used serviced in post-school education. Some of the most experienced and effective helpers are to be found among counsellors, who will be available to work with your anxiety and any of the life circumstances that fuel it. You can find more information from the Association for Student Counselling (see **Further Reading and Help**) and by asking in your local colleges and universities.

Alternative health approaches
There are many other alternative medical approaches that can be of immense help to your management of anxiety. Among these would certainly be included acupuncture, aromatherapy (the use of smelling oils in therapy) and reflexology. To find a safe and effective practitioner, consult the professional associations and listen out for personal recommendations from people whose opinions you trust.

Seeking medical help
The whole of this book is devoted to strategies to help you cope with coursework and examinations by drawing on your own resources and those of your friends and relatives around you. However there may be times when you feel so overwhelmed with anxiety that you feel permanently stressed and are exhibiting symptoms such as sickness, diarrhoea, loss of sleep and appetite. In such circumstances a visit to your doctor is highly appropriate.

Visiting your doctor
You may find someone with whom you can talk over how you are feeling and the symptoms you are experiencing. If your school, college or university does not have a counselling service, which hopefully it does, you may have the option of being referred to a practice counsellor or a psychologist to help you by talking through your concerns.

The doctor may also choose to prescribe some medication which is non-addictive. You may also have the choice of approaching a number of alternative practitioners, one of which is a homeopath or homeopathic GP (general practitioner).

Homeopathic help
'Homeopathy offers a safe alternative as its treats the whole person – the physical as well as the emotional – and therefore plays an important role in the movement back to more holistic approach to health' writes Miranda Castro in her book *The Complete Homeopathic Handbook*.

One of the remedies homeopaths may prescribe for exam problems is Argent Nitz. It will not be prescribed routinely; you will most probably have to be trembling with nervous excitement, suffering from diarrhoea and having impulsive thoughts tormenting you. The homeopath will take into account all the symptoms, the situation and you, before prescribing.

Details of how to find a homeopath near you are included in the **Further Reading and Help** section at the back of the book.

Suck a sweet. . .

Sucking a sweet or chewing gum is used by many candidates in the exam room. The easiest way to keep saliva in your mouth is to suck on a sweet. Glucose is particularly good and many students I know suck mints; checking with the college canteen on the morning of one exam, it was Polos that were the top seller.

The key point is to keep saliva in your mouth with or without a sweet. By keeping saliva in your mouth you are helping yourself to keep fears at bay.

. . . or carry a talisman

The talis is an object to which luck, safety or wonderful things are linked. If you have a small object such as a pebble that you can carry with you and touch or rub or associate with well being, it can be extremely helpful around exam times. You could use it in between and alongside revising sessions. You can also carry it with you on your journey to the exam room and have it with you in the examination room, placing it on your desk or keeping it in a pocket.

A friend gave me a piece of light green marble from Ireland which I use in this way. It had been beautifully smoothed into an oval shape with concave dips in each surface. The Irish call it a worry stone. I find it helpful to carry into new or stressful situations whether or not I look at it or touch its smooth surface. It acts as a source of reassurance and that is the essence of the idea of a talis.

You can create your own talis, even having more than one, in case one is mislaid.

SOME BASIC GUIDELINES

This section gives guidelines to both students and their helpers (other students, friends, parents, spouses and others).

Throughout, it emphasises the importance of *negotiating help* with another person. That is, not demanding it or forcing it upon others but requesting and offering. In practical terms, this means that the helper asks questions like:

'Is there anything I can do to help?'

It also means that the student asks questions like:

'Could you help me with . . .?'

It also means that the answer to both these questions could be 'No', at least initially, and that the times and conditions for help have to be discussed. Helpers can state clearly what they are prepared to offer in the way of help. Students can state equally clearly their needs (when they know what they are); helpers can help them discover their needs where they are unclear.

Helpful and unhelpful things for helpers to say

I have asked students which things their parents, friends or other helpers say which are most helpful and which are most unhelpful. They say:

Unhelpful   *Do you agree?*
It's not worth worrying about.
Cheer up.
Have you finished yet?
Pull yourself together.
You've just got to get down to it/
You must get down to it.
Get a grip on yourself.

Do some work and you'll feel better.
You can only do your best.
Don't worry.
It will be all right on the day.
Have your done your home work tonight?
Your brother/sister/cousin/friend etc.
never had this problem . . .
Others . . .

Helpful   *Do you agree?*
Is there anything I can do to help?
How's it going?
Do you want any help with anything?
How are you feeling about things?
Let me know if I can help in any way.
You seem to be working hard/You are
finding it difficult to get down to it . . .
I'll test you on that topic if you want.
Others . . .

Features of these comments and questions
They tend to be open questions, offering, without forcing, help. They accept the student's feelings.

You may find some items in 'Unhelpful' list, helpful and vice versa. It does not matter. It is important that you negotiate with your helper(s) so that they know what is helpful to you and what is not.

Working with students and friends

In the early days of schooling, you may often have felt as if you were cheating if you worked with other students on the same question. Working with others can be immensely useful, of course, and the following guidelines are designed to ensure the maximum usefulness.

- Work on each other's strengths, ie the topics you know best, are most interested in, etc.
- Constructively support each other by listening attentively; telling friends when they have been helpful; avoiding anxiety-provoking topics.
- Cooperate. Use any competitiveness to the benefit of all rather than the detriment of individuals. Don't try to elevate your own self-confidence at the expense of others (you will find fellow students who try this at exam time).
- Make group decisions binding on each member of the group. If you have voluntarily, without being placed under any duress, agreed to

do something, you must answer to the group if you have not done so.

- Form groups to practise particular techniques, eg *relaxation technique; visualisation* for relaxation. Meet regularly and help each other.

Guidelines for helpers

- Work through the book yourself, familiarising yourself, in particular, with the parts that are of direct interest and concern to the student.
- Work through the book with the student, agreeing which parts.
- Try to avoid imposing your own anxieties on to the student when the student is feeling anxious. Discuss these *either* with another person *or* with the student when the student is less anxious and wants to listen *or* both.
- Don't expect the student to be working solidly through the revision and examination period because that would be an inefficient studying approach, as is explained in this book.
- Say clearly what you are prepared to offer in the way of help.
- The essence of helpful listening is that you are attentive and accept what the student says, without moralising or judging. By keeping their confidences to yourself, you enable them to express exactly how they feel, think and behave, without comparing them with others.

Guidelines for parents

Don Davies, author of *Maximising Examination Performance* (see **Further Reading and Help** for details) gave these guidelines for parents in a *Guardian* newspaper feature on exam stress in April 1993. Here they appear with some small amendments and some page references to parts of this book which give emphasis to his points or provide more information.

- Be on the lookout for common signs of stress such as trouble sleeping, emotional mood changes, loss of appetite, skin ailments, and stomach upsets.
- Be patient, controlled and calm in the run-up to exams. Anxiety is catching.
- Adopt a realistic attitude towards your children's abilities. Don't expect too much, but be positive and emphasise academic success rather than failures.
- Avoid comparisons with successful friends or relatives. Praise commitment as well as success and try to put the exams in perspective: they are not the be-all and end-all. Show interest in their achievements outside school work.
- Make sure there is a place available at home where the student can

work alone (see pp 25-27).
- In extreme cases of stress seek professional help (see pp 143-145).
- Avoid offering rewards such as money, clothes or cars. Young people may feel they are being manipulated, and it might stop them developing an interest in the subject for its own sake.
- Above all, make it clear that your son or daughter is valued for reasons entirely unconnected with academic progress.
- Read **Helpful and unhelpful things for helpers to say** (pp 146-147) and spot your most helpful sayings.

TALK ABOUT YOUR PROBLEM

Ask your helper to be an attentive listener for you. Negotiate the kind of help you would like. Here are two suggestions for you to consider.

Listen without speaking

Ask your partner to say nothing, simply give you their undivided attention. Ask them to encourage you to talk by non-verbal signals, eg smiles, nods, eye contact, touch, and to allow you to display any emotion you feel.

Talk for as little or as long as you like about any aspect of the problem that is uppermost in your mind. You could use parts of the book to give a focus to what you say, if you prefer. The exercise will give you an opportunity to listen to yourself. At the end, you could summarise the main concerns you have expressed.

Listen and summarise

Use the above negotiated approach, asking your helper to be equally attentive and encouraging to you. This time, leave pauses in what you say and express, for your helper to summarise both the fact and the feeling in what you have said. If the helper doesn't summarise the essential meaning of what you have said, help by repeating what you expressed and giving your helper another chance to summarise it, in turn. Continue, using this approach, until you have been able to express all of the problem.

Tackling the problem

Use your helper to work through the four stages of the **Tackling the problem** exercise by using either of the approaches from these two *Listening* exercises. The helper works with you, one stage at a time, to enable you to clarify what you can do about it and how you are going to do so. You could use the same approach to talk through the **Hierarchy of anxiety**.

Using revision cards with a partner

Draw a diagram, make up a spider or patterned note card(s) or construct some linear key word notes.

Revise the card(s) for 15 or 20 minutes (at most). Re-check that you understand and can recall all of the card(s) contents.

Teach your partner about the topic, allowing – and encouraging – questions about the topic. When a point is unclear, stop and explain it. Work through the topic until you have both completed it to your satisfaction *or* have agreed to meet again to continue.

Using your partner to fire questions

Work for a set period in your work room, eg ½ to 1 hour. Then ask your cooperative partner to fire questions at you about the topic. It will obviously help if the partner had some knowledge about the topic or a clear indication of what to ask. However, what you are seeking from this exercise is to keep flexible and alert to surprise questions and fresh angles are a bonus from this method.

'Test me'

An additional option for the **Basic revision method** is to explain what you have been reading and learning to your partner. Alternatively, pass your partner your notes and ask to be tested on your understanding. 'Test me' is one of the commonest forms of using others as helpers and is as useful as it ever was.

USING MORE THAN ONE HELPER FOR REVISION

Conducting a seminar

One person in a group of 3, 4, 5 or 6, explains a topic to others. They can then ask questions, debate your points, give their own ideas, etc.

This technique has been very successful for a number of students I know and is highly recommended by them.

You can use this idea of marking and commenting on each other's work in a number of ways:

- on presentations to a seminar.

- on introductions or conclusions to a topic, written or spoken.

- on the clarity and evidence of revision notes, particularly **Key word revision cards** (NB most cards are prepared for yourself. They may need amendment for presentation to others).

- on short, or outline answers to questions. A photocopy of each, marked silently, marks announced and then discussed, is particularly effective. (Examiners use the same techniques when they meet at Standardisation meetings to ensure they are marking in the same way, to the same standard and have grasped all the points for which marks may be awarded.)

Brainstorming

Choose a topic or question which has a large number of aspects to it. Questions involving solutions, consequences, results or which ask you to offer explanations are particularly appropriate.

In your group, negotiate for one person to record information for the group. This may be on a tape recorder, a linear note form or patterned notes on a large sheet of paper or a piece of A4 paper. The recorder has the essential role of recording every point made by other group members.

Each member of the group, including the recorder, now has the opportunity to offer their solutions, explanations, etc. The ideas should come as quickly as possible. All of them must be recorded no matter how absurd or funny another group member may find them. No member of the group is allowed to criticise another member's ideas. The recorder should intervene if this happens and stop the rule breaker. Once all the ideas are recorded (the recorder can give interim summaries of what has been written down if this method is being used) the whole list can be opened up for debate and criticism and evaluation. In this way, all the ideas have been heard before any evaluation occurs and a wider perspective has been thrown on the question.

Giving a five-minute lecture

Prepare your topic by listing the major points you would wish to make in answer to a question. Talk about them, briefly, without elaboration, detail, detour or examples for exactly five minutes.

Invite your group to ask questions. Each member may ask only one question at a time, in turn. You should make your answers brief – one word, one phrase, one sentence answers. The object is to maximise participation and to generate a large number of questions and thus stimulate every member's thinking about the topic.

Form your own revision group

One mature student, Tilly, was a member of a seminar group on the second year of her degree course. They were extremely helpful to each other, forming a revision group and tackling topics together in the period before the exam.

A prize winning student in Trinidad worked as part of a group of eight students throughout the revision session and attributed part of her success to the group.

Both groups used the approaches mentioned both in this chapter and in Chapters Three and Four.

Pool your questions

When you meet as a group, one idea is to agree that you will say what individual questions you are concerned to tackle. As it is important to frame your concerns as questions, not just as 'worries', everybody may need to say what their worry-of-the-moment is and then be asked to frame it as a question.

As each question is asked in turn, others give you their ideas, suggestions or answers to the question. You can make the best use of the time if everybody listens to the answers to someone else's question (which may be equally relevant to their own). Make sure everybody has the chance to have their questions heard, even if they do not immediately get fully answered. You and they can always have another go next time you meet.

Glossary

Assignment Any task given to you to complete as part of a course. It will usually be marked and the outcome count in some way towards your final assessment for the year.

Brainstorming A way of tackling a problem either in a group or individually, which encourages the widest range of ideas to hammer out, without criticism. The process of evaluating their usefulness comes later.

BTEC The Business and Technology Education Council acts as an examining body for a wide range of vocationally-oriented courses at further and higher education levels in the early 1990s.

Continuous assessment The process of gaining marks from a course other than by examination. Assessment can both give you a guide to your progress and count towards your final year result. Can be tests, essays, reports, projects. Can also be combined with exams.

Coursework Any assignments or tasks you set yourself to do either in college, school or at home. In school it is often referred to as 'homework' when it is not completed in class time.

Deadline A date or time of day by which a piece of coursework, project or assignment is required to be repeated.

Dissertation A major written assignment often completed in later, particularly final, years of undergraduate courses of study. Usually a substantial piece of work involving some information-gathering or survey. Can also be undertaken in post graduate study.

GCSE General Certificate of Secondary Education.

Kinaesthetic The sense of touch, feel and movement.

Neuro-linguistic programming A method and process for discovering the patterns, skills and techniques used by outstanding individuals in any field to achieve outstanding results.

Professional courses Specialist Training Courses at various levels, including post graduate level, designed to produce greater levels of vocational competence as well as to update skills and know-how.

Project Any usually larger assignment which involves some investigation, information-gathering or creative design on your part.

RSA Royal Society of Arts, a long established body involved in the development of a wide range of skills in learning and in competence.

Seminar Traditionally an opportunity for a small group to discuss issues raised by one member of the group, in the form of a 'paper' on a topic or a presentation. A tutor is present who may choose to take a large or small part each week. The 'small' group may consist of over twenty-five people on some courses, but hopefully it would be between ten and fifteen at most.

Synthesis A fusing together of different senses, ideas or skills into a whole.

TEC Training and Enterprise Councils are responsible on a regional basis for effective training in the 1990s.

Undergraduate Anyone studying for a first degree, BA, BSc, BEng, BEd and so on, as well as someone studying for a Higher Diploma (although they are also termed Diplomates).

Workshop There tends to be two ways in which this word is used. One is to describe a place where creative design or fabrication takes place in arts and technology fields. The other is to describe a meeting in which you will be asked to participate in practical ways such as talking in pairs, writing down ideas, dramatising events or learning practical relaxation techniques.

Bibliography

Acres, D. and Seymour, R. *General Studies Study Guide*. Longman, 1987.

Bird, C. and Bird D.M. *Learning to Study More Effectively*. New York. Appleton Century-Crofts, 1945, pp. 195-8.

Dryden, Wendy. 'Examination Anxiety – What the Student Counsellor Can Do'. *British Journal of Guidance and Counselling*, Vol. 6, No. 2, July, 1978.

Fulwiser, T. (Ed.). *The Journal Book*. Portsmouth NH. Boynton/Cook, 1987.

Gibb, G. *Teaching Students to Learn. A student-centred approach*. Milton Keynes. Open University Press,1981.

Hamblin, D. H. *Teaching Study Skills*. Oxford. Blackwell, 1981.

Holt, John. *Learning all the time – how small children begin to read, write, count and investigate the world without being taught*. Education Now Publishing Cooperative Ltd. P O Box 186, Ticknall, Derbyshire, DE7 1WF. ISBN 1 871526 04 3.

Howe, Michael J.A. (Ed.). *Encouraging the Development of Exceptional Skills and Talents*. BPS, St Andrews House, 48, Princess Road East, Leicester LE1 7DR.

Mace, C. A. *The Psychology of Study*. London. Penguin Books (revised ed.), 1962.

Michelbaum, D. 'Self-Instruction Methods (How to do it)' in Goldstein, A. and Kaufer, F. (Eds.). *Helping People Change: Methods and Materials*, New York. Pergamon Press, 1975.

O'Connor, J. and Seymour, J. *Introducing Neuro-Linguistic Programming*. London. Mandala, 1990.

Rose, Colin. *Accelerated Learning*. Accelerated Learning Systems Ltd. Fifth Education 1991.

Seymour, R. and Acres, D. *General and Liberal Studies: A Teacher's Handbook*. London. Darton Longman and Todd, 1974.

Steffert, Dr Beverley. 'Memory'. *Counselling*. November 1993. British Association for Counselling.

Tabberer, R. and Allman, J. 'Study Skills at 16 plus.' *Research in Progress*, No. 4, NFER, 1981.

Wilby, Peter. 'How to win at exams – all you really need to know'. London. *Sunday Times Colour Supplement*, 16 May 1982, pp. 26-38.

Further Reading and Help

BOOKS

Acres, D. *How to Survive at College*. How To Books 1987. A comprehensive guide to all aspects of coping with life in higher education.

Ansell, Gwen. *Make the Most of Your Memory*. National Extension College 1984. Looks at all aspects of memory in a clear, practical way.

Ashman, S. and George A. *Study and Learn*. London. Heinemann 1982. The best book on studying available at present. Highly recommended.

Barnes, R. *Successful Study for Degrees*. Routledge 1992. One of a number of books recommended by students as being helpful.

Bourner T. and Race, P. *How to Win as a Part-Time Student*. Kogan Page 1990. For those tackling study in what can be a very difficult way, a helpful book to guide you through.

Bowness, Charles. *The Practice of Meditation*. Aquarian Press 1979. A useful book with a lot of meditative techniques to help you unwind.

Buzan, Tony. *Use Your Head*. London. BBC Publications 1989. Very good on creative patterns and certain kinds of memorising.

Buzan, Tony. *Use Your Memory*. BBC Publications, 1987. Chapter by chapter of different memory approaches for different situations. Comprehensive and, generally, comprehensible.

Castro, Miranda. *The Complete Homeopathy Handbook*. Macmillan. Available by post from The Homeopathic Supply Co., Fairview, 4 Nelson Road, Sheringham, Norfolk NR26 8BU.

Chapman, David, *GCSEs: surviving the course*. Dextral Books. Practical tips on tackling GCSEs.

Cocker, D. *Successful Examination Techniques*. Northcote House 1987. Specific detailed guidelines on examination techniques.

Davies, Don. *Maximising Examination Performance: A Psychological*

156

Approach. Kogan Page 1986. This book reports the result of a survey of stress related problems of post-A level students, and suggests some ways to do the psychological preparation for exams.

Dunleavy, P. *Studying for a Degree – in the Humanities and Social Sciences*. Macmillan 1986. A very detailed and helpful book for some of the detailed issues of studying especially in writing critically and structuring work.

Edwards, Betty. *Drawing on the Right Side of the Brain*. Souvenir Press 1981. Looks at ways of using the creative, free-flowing mental faculties and includes some very helpful ideas, together with a step-by-step course.

Fairbairn, G. and Winch, C. *Reading, Writing and Reasoning: A Guide for Students*. Open University Press 1991. Another book recommended to me by students as a help to improving the analysis of a question and the quality of argument.

Freeman, R. *Mastering Study Skills*. Macmillan 1982. Includes some useful guidelines on thinking and arguing effectively.

Hennessy, B. *How to Write an Essay*. How To Books 1994.

Lorayne, H. *Improve Exam Results in 30 days*. Thorsons 1992. Some highly specific and wide ranging memory tips on such issues as learning formulae.

Madders, J. *Stress and Relaxation: Self-Help Techniques for Everyone*. (1988 edition). Macdonald Optima.

Marshall, L. and Rowland, F. *Guide to Learning Independently*. OU Press 1993. A useful all-round study guide with useful chapters on dissertations.

Meredeen, S. *Study for Survival and Success*. Paul Chapman 1988. How to cope with the whole of being at college with some helpful guidelines.

Northedge, A. *Good Study Guide*. OU Press 1990. An excellent general resource about study skills aimed primarily at adults.

O'Connor, J. and Seymour, J. *Introducing Neuro-Linguistic Programming*. London. Mandala, 1990.

Race, P. and Bourner, T. *How to Win as a Part-Time Student: Study Skills Guide*. Kogan Page 1990. Another useful guide for the part-time student.

Rose, Colin. *Accelerated Learning*. Accelerated Learning Systems Ltd. Fifth edition 1991.

Rowntree, D. *Learn How to Study*. London. MacDonald (Revised edition). 1976. One of the best books published on studying techniques in recent years. A programmed text. Very good guidelines on taking examinations.

Smith, P. *How to Write an Assignment*. How To Books 1994.

Whale, John. *Put it in Writing*. Dent 1984.

AUDIO/VIDEO TAPES AND FURTHER HELP

Acres, David. *David Acres answers your questions about 'How to Pass Exams Without Anxiety'*. Audio Tapes and Guidance available from Marjon Learning Support, College of St Mark & St John, Derriford Road, Plymouth PL6 8BH.

Association for Student Counselling, c/o British Association for Counselling, 1 Regent Place, Rugby, Warwickshire CV21 2PJ. Tel: (0788) 550899. For locating counselling help in college and university.

Davies, Don. *How to Conquer Exam Nerves: Maximising Examination Performance*. Available by post from Performance Programmes, 16a Priory Road, Malvern, Worcester WR14 3DR. This 64-minute tape covers test anxiety; anxiety stress and performance; learning to relax; developing confidence; improving concentration and increasing efficiency.

Letts Study Guides: GCSE; A/AS Level; Languages – including audio cassettes. A series of commercially produced GCSE and A Level study packs can help with individual subjects.

'Lingo'. Examines how to learn a language. BBC Publications 1991.

Longman Revise Guides, GCSE and A Level.

Longman GCSE Pass Packs. Using an audiotape plus booklet on subjects like English, Physics etc.

Locke, Dr. *Overcoming Examination Nerves – Successful Studying*. Therapeutic Visualisation Ltd, 6 Milton Road, Bentley Heath B93 8AA. Teaches how to manage stress and remain calm. Pleasant music and voice for deep relaxation to instil a calm and confident manner.

Rose, Colin and Goll, Louise. *Accelerate Your Learning*. Accelerated Learning Systems Ltd, 60 Aylesbury Road, Aston Clinton, Aylesbury, Buckinghamshire, England produce an excellent Study Guide as well as packs of material to learn languages. Printed, audio and video materials of high quality.

Society of Homeopaths, 2 Artizan Road, Northampton NN1 4HU. Tel: (0604) 21400.

Index

abbreviations, 59-60
ability, 13-14
achievement, 14-15
answers (*see* questions)
anxiety, 107-145
association (*see* memory)
audio-tape, 51, 63, 72, 79

brain, right and left halves, 61, 68-69, 73
brain patterns, creative (*see* notes)
brainstorming, 151
breathing techniques (*see* relaxation)
brief tips, 19, 40, 62, 84, 108, 113

colours, 27, 31-33, 58, 68, 140
computers, 37-38
concentration, 24-25
'Corpse, the', 127-128
counselling, 143-144
coursework, 18-42

deadlines, 36-37
determination, 13-14
diary, 50
dissertation, 28-29
dyslexic students, 31-32

essays, 100-102
exam 'nerves', 87, 89-92, 116-118
examinations, 83-106, 117-118
    oral exams, 103-104

feelings, 17, 110, 147
filing, 26-27, 35

folders, 27
friends, 76, 124–126, 147, 148

GANNT chart, 33
GCSE, 11, 18-29
Gestalt idea, 30

hard work, 13-14
health, 86, 144-145
help, 38, 144
helpers, 21, 146-152
hierarchies,
    revision, 41-45
    anxiety, 111-112

imagination, 77, 80, 140-141
interest, 41-45, 111-112

journal, learning, 27-28

key word revision card, 47, 57-59, 150
key words, 96-97

lectures,
    five minute, 151
    notes, 46-48
legibility, 27, 104-105
libraries, 37, 41
listening,
    focussed, 143
    importance of, 149
    to music, 51, 125-126
lists, 44, 110-112

mathematics, 80-82

memory, 61-82
   association, 63, 79
   facts, 77-82
   mnemonics, 77-78
   repetition, 63
   testing, 63-64
motivation, 14, 21-23, 29, 50-54
multiple choice (*see* questions)

negative,
   attitudes, 89-92, 115
   self-statements, 116
   symbols, 41-43
neuro-linguistic programming, 61
notebook, 50
notes,
   filing, 26-28
   patterned, 10-11, 48-49, 97
   spider, 47, 97
   use in revision, 46-48

objective tests (*see* questions)
outline answers, 80, 94-97

panic (*see* anxiety)
parents, 11, 148-149
past experience, 110
performance, 13-15, 88-89, 105-106
photograph album, 32
portfolios, 27
positive,
   attitudes, 22-23, 114-116
   symbols, 77
Post-Its, 30
problems,
   tackling, 150
   talking about, 149-150
projects, 28-29

questions,
   analysing your questions, 10-11
   around a topic, 8-9, 46
   importance of, 8-11, 25-26
   multiple choice, 102-103
   objective, 102-103
   practice answers to, 80, 88
   spotting, 45-46
   types of, 8-9, 83-84, 98-104

   underlining key words in, 11, 96-97

reading,
   with questioning approach, 8-14, 56
   the exam paper, 94-95
relaxation,
   breathing, 128-131
   emergency, 128
   muscular, 131-139
   rest and relax, 23, 52-53, 124-125
   visualisation, 139-143
remembering (*see* memory)
revision, 39-60, 151-152

science and technology subjects, 80
self statements, 116-118
seminars, 150-151
senses, using, 69-77, 81
simulation, 88, 140-141
sleep, 53, 79, 123-128
spelling, 78-79, 105
stress, 113-121
summarising, 56-60, 149
symbol system, 31, 41-43, 100

talisman, 145
testing, 63-64, 150
television, 26, 28, 51, 72
time, use of,
   in coursework, 21-37
   in exams, 94-96, 104
   in revision, 51-54
topics,
   spotting, 41
   subjects and symbols, 41-43
tutors, 29-30, 146

understanding, 63

variety, 25, 50, 120
visualisation, 71, 139-143
visual recall, 75-77

waking, 93, 121-122
where to revise, 50-51, 120-121
where to study, 25-26
work rate, 14
worry (*see* anxiety)